Sandy

Sandy

by

C Richard Toye

THE STORY OF A BOY AND HIS
FRIENDS GROWING UP IN CORNWALL
IN THE LATE 1800s

GREAT WESTERN BOOKS

First published in 2003 by Great Western Books
Loundshay Manor Cottage
Preston Bowyer, Milverton
Somerset TA4 1QF
www.amolibros.co.uk

Distributed by Gazelle Book Services Limited
Falcon House, Queen Square
Lancaster, England LA1 1RN

British Library Cataloguing in Publication Data
A catalogue record for this book is available from the British Library

ISBN 0 9543711 0 0

Typeset by Amolibros, Watchet, Somerset
This book production has been managed by Amolibros
Printed and bound by T J International Ltd, Padstow, Cornwall

Acknowledgements

I wish to thank the following for their help in the preparation of this book:

Staffs of the Cornish Public Libraries and Cornwall Maritime Museum;

P Gilson, retired Master of Falmouth Grammar School;

A Campbell, Ship Historian;

Anne Weatherston;

To my wife Margaret for help and patience during the preparation of this book.

'There is always one moment in childhood when the door opens and lets the future in.'

Graham Greene, *The Power and the Glory*, 1940

About the author

BORN IN Plymouth Charles Toye did a shipwright apprenticeship in Devonport and Rosyth Dockyards. He was in numerous managerial posts for the Ministry of Defence, one of which included a tour of duty in Gibraltar. He studied at Strathclyde University and gained a First Class Honours degree in Naval Architecture

After two years as a marine surveyor for the Board of Trade at Belfast he returned to the MOD as a Naval Constructor at Rosyth Dockyard with duty at Swan Hunters Newcastle and finally at Rosyth Dockyard.

He is now retired and living with his wife and family in Fife.

Sandy's father settles in Falmouth town

SANDY WAS born in a house in Killigrew Street, Falmouth, on the 21st of April 1877. He was christened Charles Peter Toye and was the second son of John and Elizabeth Toye. Sandy, his nickname, he got because of his reddish-brown hair. He had two brothers. Joseph, the eldest, was born in 1874, and Frederick, the youngest, arrived in the world in 1883. In the late nineteenth century Cornwall was relatively prosperous, and Sandy grew up when its people thrived on a vibrant fishing and boat-building industry, and when there were still profitable tin mines dotted about the county.

His father came from farming stock and grew up on a hillside farm near Budock, a concern that his Uncle Benjamin one day inherited. When that happened, it seemed that John had the choice of either finding other work or staying on as a farm hand. Fortunately, his father had foreseen precisely this problem, and so had made arrangements for John to be apprenticed to a cabinet-maker. That was in Falmouth, the town John eventually moved to, having served his apprenticeship and qualified as a cabinet-maker in his own right.

It was after he'd worked in the town for several years that he met and married Elizabeth Richards, the daughter of a miner destined to be captain one day of one of the local tin mines. They set up home in Killigrew Street (where, as I have said, Sandy was born). Soon after that John set up his own joinery business. He also worked a small holding near to home, and here he grew vegetables.

Sandy's first day at infants' school

ONE DAY, when Sandy was five, at a time of year that brought the changing colours of autumn, his parents enrolled him for school. The one they chose was the Trevethen Board School. Having talked it over with the master, it was agreed that Sandy would start in September. The year was 1882.

The Trevethen school was at the corner of Ersey and Tresavona Terraces, with the building itself only newly constructed (in fact the school was established in 1879). It was large for its times, having 280 boys and 160 girls. School staffing consisted of one qualified male teacher – the master – and one qualified female, who was mistress to the girls. To assist them were pupil teachers and monitors. Pupil teachers were uncertified, and so received tuition from their qualified peers – usually amounting to an hour per weekday after school hours. Their aim was to sit an exam and so qualify as fully trained teachers themselves. With those limitations, the master and mistress were invariably overworked, with many large classes to teach. That meant that, much of the time, teaching of some classes was in the hands of the pupil teachers and monitors, and that had implications for the quality of education as well as general discipline.

Naturally, Sandy's first day at school was daunting enough, what with getting up early, and all the ritual of washing, dressing and breakfasting to schedule. It didn't much help that he knew other children starting on the same day, because it was all such a frightening experience. He and his mother set out along Killigrew Street, and could soon see on the slope of the moor, sliding inescapably into view, the dreaded school. There it was, in all its fearful glory, with its whitewashed walls and enormous windows, nestling between New Market Inn and Trevethen Hall. Shudder.

He looked on forlornly when his mother chatted briefly with the master, who in the shadow of the main entrance passed him over to one of the pupil teachers. He was led away, in mixed terror and anticipation, and at the end of a long gloomy corridor was told to take off his coat and leave it on a bench. He noticed there were chairs stacked in the corners.

Next he was led to a large room with a very high ceiling, and walls that were stark and bare and forbidding. Today though was cold and wet, and a fire burning in the grate cheered him a little, as it did the other new arrivals. The teacher told them all to sit, and indicated the row upon row of benches arranged regimentally in the classroom. He gave them slates and chalks and began his lesson (paper and books at that time were expensive and in short supply) – the first exercise being to copy words from the blackboard. Spelling was the goal.

'Welcome to Standard I,' he said cheerfully. 'What I want to hear from you now is the sound of chalk on slate.' He wrote some simple words on the blackboard, and was soon helping the slower ones, mouthing the syllables for them to repeat, and correcting pronunciation. When they were all exhausted from that, he read them a story. When that too was over he sent them off for their midday break and a welcome bite to eat.

In the afternoon they were allowed to play with building blocks, and little wooden shapes that vaguely resembled animals he knew. Here Sandy paused often, able to hear the class next door, where the teacher had got her charges chanting their times tables. Sandy's day ended before theirs, the youngest class finishing earlier than those of the older children. When his mother came to collect him, he couldn't wait to get back home, eager to tell the whole family all about his very first day at school.

Sandy's new friends

SANDY SETTLED down well in Standard I, and in his time as an infant got good results, which saw him progress to the higher classes. A year ahead of him were Tom Richards and Jim Earle, a difference that didn't stop the three becoming good friends. They already knew each other out of school, because Sandy's father had done joinery work at the Richards' farm near Falmouth, and was often employed by Jim's dad too, with his fishing boats and warehouse on the harbour. Sandy always went with his dad on these outings, and that's how he got to know Jim and Tom. However, because he was younger, and wasn't in their class at school, they didn't immediately become close friends. It took a few years.

School progress

SANDY WORKED steadily in Standard I and II, and with a bit of effort and help from his older brother Joe got himself a good grounding during these two years, in the three Rs particularly. In Standard III it was much the same, though now the days dragged, much of what they did being by rote and repetition – especially where the times tables were concerned. Nevertheless, he got through Standard III with good marks in all subjects, while at the same time his brother Joe finished Standard VI and qualified for grammar school. Despite the hard work, he enjoyed reading the books that came his way, and these as well as his hobnail boots became his most treasured possessions. With these latter he in common with many of his classmates really made the sparks fly outside on the cobbled streets, running and skidding and heaven knew what else. Clumping along with their hobnails when swarming into school was another great pastime – until, that is, their teachers demanded they behave themselves.

Accident with the magic lantern show

ONE DAY that winter something very out of the ordinary happened at school. It was the last Friday at the end of January and the master suddenly announced that there was going to be a magic lantern show. In fact it was going to be that very afternoon, in the main hall.

When the time came, pupils from all classes were assembled and told which benches to use. This took some doing, of course – as a feat of organisation more than anything. Added to that, some of the older boys insisted on leaving large spaces between them when they did eventually sit (just to be awkward). In due course however everyone had a place and waited with bated breath for the show to begin.

The master introduced a man called Mr Beard, who was here to give a talk on the countries of the world, using his magic lantern. Mr Beard had placed it and its various accessories prominently by the fire, which because of the cold had been heaped with extra coals, and was blazing merrily.

All went well, except that after about half an hour Mr Beard had difficulty adjusting the settings for his slides. The problem was that the apparatus wasn't producing enough acetylene, though little did he know that what there was was leaking out and slowly building up in front of the fire. Inevitably, a live piece of coal jumped out and exploded with the gas, sending a shower of red-hot cinders everywhere, and filling the room with smoke.

Children in a panic shouted and screamed and made for the door, where their teachers ushered them out to the playground, with as little fuss as possible. Mr Beard switched off his machine, and with the master's help hauled it out of the building.

Somewhat anxiously the master gathered everyone into his or her respective classes and did a roll call, and to his very great relief found all children accounted for. At the same time his teachers and assistants went rushing back and forth with buckets of water to douse the flames, which had very quickly spread to the wooden floor. In fact this was so serious a threat that a human chain had to be formed to get the buckets in and out and re-filled with minimum delay.

In a short while — which seemed endless to the teachers — the fire was under control, though everyone was gasping under the palls of smoke. When that eventually cleared the master and some of his staff went inside to survey the extent of the damage. The floor near the fireplace was badly burnt, and the walls and ceiling were heavily charred. The water to fight the blaze was oozing everywhere. 'What a mess!' the master said. He now knew only too well what a bad state the school was in, and brought teachers and pupils together in the playground, congratulating everyone for their help and co-operation — the children with the buckets, the teachers for the way they fought the fire.

He said that, having weighed matters carefully, the school was in no fit state to continue with lessons. The cleaners would have to come in to mop the water, then he'd have to get workmen to make good the damage. For now, the infants' school was closed, and wouldn't re-open till Tuesday morning. Sandy and his friends were overjoyed. To them, it was as good as a holiday, short though that would be.

Sandy walked the short distance home, where his mother was surprised to see him back so early. She did however know about the fire, having seen great billows of smoke sailing over the housetops, though she didn't know where it was. Sandy explained. She saw the gleam in his eye when he said that school was over till Tuesday, and from now until then it was just like a holiday. She smiled. 'We shall see about that, my lad,' she said. As they were going inside Joe bowled up to the front gate, an enormous grin on his face – for he too was off till Tuesday.

Joe and Sandy discover the toils of washday

OVER THE weekend the two boys were allowed to play, provided they did their chores as usual. Little did they know what was in store for Monday. They were roused from their beds very early, with the news ringing in their ears that it was washday. 'Time to get up,' she said. 'Time to come and help your ma.' They washed and dressed and went downstairs for breakfast, after which Joe's first job was to set the fire under the copper boiler in the wash-house. In the meantime Sandy had to fetch all the blankets and flannelette sheets that his mother had stripped from the beds.

Dejected slightly, Joe went out back to the wash-house and broke up some sticks to put with the coal he'd got for the fire. When Sandy arrived with the bedclothes he helped his mother fill the copper boiler with water. These tasks over, she sent the boys back to the kitchen, where she'd prepared hot drinks and buttered scones. While they were busy with that she lit the fire and wiped the clotheslines.

When the water began to heat up, she put in the soap and stirred with a wooden paddle. When the soap had dissolved she put in the blankets, then the sheets, then sealed the boiler with its wooden lid. By now the boys had had their little feast, and were allowed to play in the garden until it was time to heave the washing out and put it through the mangle. For that job, it was they who had to turn the handle, while their mother fed the blankets and sheets through the rollers, which squeezed the water out.

The handle took all their strength, which, when moving, turned a wheel connected to a series of cogs, which, when *they* got going, rotated the three all-important wooden rollers. Once that was done, the blankets and sheets were put in baskets and taken out to the garden. There Joe and Sandy helped her hang the newly laundered bedding from the lines, secured with wooden pegs. Once that was over, it was two tired boys who went to the kitchen for lunch. Having recovered their strength, they were allowed to play in the garden for the rest of the day, quite glad they wouldn't have to help with the washing for some time to come.

Return to school

ON TUESDAY, when Sandy and Joe returned to school, there was still the smell of smoke about the place, despite the fact that all the rooms had been swept and cleaned. The painters were setting up their trestles in the main hall and were about to make good the walls and ceiling. Where the fire had started, there were two joiners ripping out the floorboards, which were soon to be replaced. Soon everything settled back to its old routine, when even the thud of hammers and the smell of paint began not to be noticed.

School games

It was not until the end of his year in Standard III – when he was older and more robust – that Sandy started to enjoy games. With the other boys he played hopscotch, five stones, tag, and – when they could afford to buy them – iron hoops, which they rolled along with iron crooks.

Girls tended to play with wooden hoops, rolling these along with wooden sticks. Mainly they played circle games, ones that involved skipping ropes and spinning tops.

The most popular games, mainly played by boys, were 'tag' and 'capture'. In the game 'tag' – sometimes called 'tig' – one person chases the others all round the playground until one of them is caught. That person then becomes the chaser.

The game similar to 'tag' but much more robust was 'capture' – or 'old man smack', as it was called in some parts of Cornwall. Here one person is the 'keeper' or 'old man', and has to stand in the middle of the playground. Meanwhile the other children have formed into two groups at opposing ends of the playground. Each group then has to run across the playground, avoiding capture by the 'keeper'. When a child *is* caught, he or she joins the keeper in the middle.

The two groups repeat their runs, so that more and more players are captured by the keepers. As more players are caught, they join hands, who then chase whoever remains in the two groups, making further captures easier and easier. The longer it goes on, the more hectic the game gets, especially now that the chasers have to ensnare the remaining players, and not just touch them. Some children, desperate to escape, would often leave bits of clothing or buttons in the hands of the chasers. When the last person is caught, he or she becomes the 'keeper' at the start of the next game.

Sandy, towards the close of Standard III year, although he played most of these games, didn't play 'capture.' It got out of hand too often, with clothing badly ripped, and too many nasty bruises from falling on the playground.

Sandy's friendships develop

BY THE time he reached Standard IV he was tall and sturdy for his age, and feeling more confident. With his father doing more joinery at the Richards' farm and at George Earle's warehouse, Sandy, when he went to these places with him, found himself further and further acquainted with Tom and Jim. Soon they were always together out of school hours, and despite the pranks they played all of them worked hard and got on well at school.

Apple scrumping

GOOD AS they were with class work, that didn't stop the trio getting into trouble. One week in the summer term the teacher in charge of Standard V was taken ill. To get over this, the pupils in Standard IV and V were put in a class together, the whole lot decamping to the main hall where there was enough room for all their desks. One afternoon, the teacher in charge of this was called away. Before departing, he left the monitor in charge, who for a while oversaw things without any problem. However, with the demands of the day and the warmth of the weather, he soon got tired – and worse than that, fell fast asleep (and this at the teacher's desk).

This being the last lesson of the day, the three friends decided to slip out, and, tiptoeing away from school, Jim, the oldest, suggested they go apple scrumping. There were a good many apple trees scattered in the gardens backing on to Killigrew Street, and that's where they headed for. The gardens here were long, with most households in that neighbourhood growing their own vegetables, as well as having fruit trees. They came in by a side path and slowly crossed the field at the back of the street, stopping at the first garden they found where they could see an abundance of apples. They climbed over the back wall then scoured the trees for the biggest fruits, and soon were filling their pockets and caps to bulging. They were sure they hadn't been seen.

Just as they started to climb the wall back to the field, there was a loud and angry shout from the house. Peter Pasco, who owned it, had caught sight of them, and here he was now rushing out after them waving a stick. Luckily they were over the wall and into the field before he could reach them. Off they ran, heads down, hoping not be recognised. Sadly for them, in the suddenness of their flight, they lost a lot of their booty, though still had plenty of apples left. At last they sat down, the panic over – and completely out of breath – and began to look at precisely what they'd got.

When they glanced back, there was Podgy Pasco, still shaking his stick at them (he'd got that nickname, being short and fat with bandy legs), though he was quite unable to give chase. His hair was long and black and curly, and his complexion was swarthy. The boys knew him as someone who sold fruit and vegetables at the local market, though they'd only ever seen him from a distance – rather as they saw him now.

Once the three boys had got their breath back, they settled down and went through their caps and pockets. The apples they'd managed to keep, and hadn't lost in the field, weren't quite ripe (they discovered). This didn't deter them. They were hungry and soon devoured most of the large ones, throwing the smaller ones away.

Having skipped off school early, the three boys made sure they got home at their usual time, and so weren't found out by their parents – for now at least.

Retribution

NEXT MORNING the situation was very different indeed, because the three boys turning up for school were all cramped with stomach ache. Those unripe apples were wreaking their worst. When they actually got in to school their pupil teacher told them to report to the master's room immediately. The boys had this dread feeling that something very unpleasant was about to happen, and guessed it had something to do with Podgy Pasco.

When they slunk into the master's room their worst fears were met. Not only had Mr Pasco reported them to the master, the monitor – when he'd eventually woken up – had seen the three were absent and reported that fact. The master was furious. The boys' parents would be told – of their absence *and* the theft. If they weren't ashamed of themselves now, they certainly would be after the six strokes of the cane he was about to administer across each of their bottoms.

Their faces red and bottoms sore, and each with a stomach ache into the bargain, the three boys left the master's room. Their lesson had been learnt. Now all they had to do was face the wrath of their parents.

Problems with a wasps' nest

When Sandy began work in Standard V, Tom and Jim likewise started in Standard VI. For the latter two, hard work was important, because the marks they got would determine whether or not they went to grammar school. That put a slight dampener on their activities, and adventures came to them less and less. However, on one occasion their curiosity got the better of them, resulting in quite an experience.

One day after school the three friends were playing in the fields behind Killigrew Street. They had had a game of hide and seek in the long grass, but were now taking a rest under the trees at the far end of the field. Among those trees was one that had been blown down in a storm, and it was on the trunk of this that they'd parked themselves. When they stopped their chatter and caught their breath all of them could hear the sound of buzzing where there were wasps in one of the surrounding trees. They followed the noise and found a nest. Tom thought he might like to find some honey and so foolishly picked up a stick and poked at the nest. That really did it – because out came not just one or two wasps, but a whole swarm of them.

The three boys took to their heels and ran as fast as they could across the field. Tom, in lagging behind the other two, was the first to get caught, and bore the brunt of the attack – though his friends didn't escape unscathed. All were badly stung. Their heads, faces, necks and arms were covered – with Tom in such bad shape that the other two had to help him home before getting their own stings treated. All of them had hugely swollen faces, which, painfully, their mothers treated with iodine. For Tom, it made him quite ill, and he developed a fever, from which it took several days to recover. For Sandy and Jim, who returned to school immediately – all they got was laughed at by the other pupils, because they had so much iodine daubed on their faces, necks and arms. They were called the 'monsters from the moor' for days on end, and saw the teasing stop only when the iodine had completely washed off and the swellings were down.

It certainly taught the three boys one important thing about wasps – not to go interfering with their nests.

Sandy prepares for grammar school

SANDY, BY the time he was in Standard VI, knew he would have to work hard to gain good passes for grammar school. Greatly to his advantage was a settled home life, and the fact that his brother Joe helped him with his studies.

The Earle family moves to Mawnan Smith

TOM AND Jim started their own lives at grammar school in the September of 1887. In that same year Jim also moved to a new house. His father had been looking for a plot of land within five miles of his business in Falmouth, where he wanted to build a new place for his family. The main reason for this was the deterioration in his wife's health, who suffered badly from bronchitis, an ailment exacerbated by the increase in dirt and smoke from the new factories near to where they presently lived.

He found the plot he wanted near Mawnan Smith, tucked away in the countryside well away from the factories and mines. The plot was sufficient to build a large house and workshop, and here he could also undertake some of his minor boat repairs. The site was about three miles from Falmouth – near enough that Jim could be taken to and collected from school in the horse and trap. One other advantage was the proximity of Porth Navas, where Jim's father had a boat slip. Here his craftsmen carried out repairs to the smaller fishing boats he owned. His fishing was in Helford Passage waters.

The family moved into the newly built house in the spring time, where the clean country air helped to reduce Mrs Earle's bronchitis. Jim of course did miss his friends in Falmouth, but knew he would always be able to visit them using the new pony and cart his father had just acquired. And as, too, Helford Passage was safe fishing, Jim persuaded his father to let him use one of the small boats at weekends.

Sandy's father inherits his uncle's farm

TOWARDS THE end of Sandy's year in Standard VI, his father received news that his old Uncle Benjamin had died. Shortly after that came a letter from his uncle's solicitor, asking for a meeting on the Monday afternoon at two o'clock. This was for the reading of the will. At that meeting, he met his cousin Alice Toye, whom he had not seen for many years. She was living in Penzance, but apart from that they hadn't been particularly friendly over the past years. Alice was a middle-aged spinster, short, plump, with fair hair and rosy cheeks.

A clerk – stocky, ruddy faced and bald – ushered them into the solicitor's sanctum, a place dark and gloomy and filled with heavy oak furniture. The books on the shelves had several layers of dust. On the floor near the desk were dozens of legal documents, all tied up with different coloured ribbons.

The solicitor introduced himself as Mr Tremain. He was tall and had a stoop, with hair that was black and grizzled. His features were pale and he wore a black moustache. He produced the will and read its preliminary content, before getting to the main business. A large sum of money and a few ornaments were bequeathed to Alice, while the farm and stock were left to John.

There were some smaller sums of money for the farm hands. John couldn't believe his good fortune, particularly when he had never got on well with his uncle, who was a bachelor. Uncle Benjamin had never seemed to have much interest in John or his family.

Once Tremain had concluded matters he handed over the keys and deeds for the farm, John Toye thanking him profusely. He said goodbye to his cousin Alice and left the room feeling quite elated, and hardly believing what had happened. He floated home in a kind of dream.

When Sandy heard the news, he wanted to know where exactly the farm was. His father said it was close to the Richards' place, which of course pleased Sandy no end. John had some work to do that day – an urgent repair to a house in Kimberley Park Road – but the following evening they would all be able to visit the farm.

The Toye family visits the new home

ON THAT next evening Sandy's mother tidied up the kitchen quickly after their meal, John having got home early. The plan was to spend as much time as possible at the farm before it got dark. John got out the horse and wagon from the stable, and the family all climbed up for the two-mile drive or so to the farm. The journey took between ten and fifteen minutes, by which time they were all eager to explore. The bad news was that the farm and farmhouse were in a bad state of repair. The wooden entrance gate was broken, and lay in pieces in the grass. Slates were missing from all the roofs – outbuildings included. The farmhouse did however look a sturdy building, constructed of stone, with two floors and a soaring ridge, though the vegetable garden was overgrown, its produce shot and strewn with weeds.

Sandy's mother went in first. She found papers and clothes in heaps in the hall, and the rooms covered in dust. All the windows were very dirty. The rest of the family followed her in and all soon found themselves in the kitchen. Here it was reasonably clean, but untidy, with ashes still in the grate under the coal range, whose brass-work and fender were a dirty green with verdigris. The curtains were old and torn.

Next they tried the parlour. This too was reasonably clean, but again it was untidy – with coats and other clothes thrown on the chairs. This had been the room most used by their deceased uncle. Adjacent to that was a bathroom, clean but with curtains old and worn. There were numerous cupboards downstairs, all littered with more clothes and lots of old boots. In one of them John found some tools, all in a fairly good state, some not having yet been removed from their boxes.

There were four bedrooms upstairs, and a room with a toilet and hand basin. The bedrooms were all of different sizes, with two of them looking out over the hills. The largest had been their uncle's – his clothes were still hanging up in a cupboard, and his dressing gown was draped over a chair. There was a large bed and other bits of furniture, and there was a mirror on the wall next to the bed. The bed was fitted with a mattress but the bedding had been removed.

Sandy chose a small back bedroom as his own, as it looked out over the hills. Joe and young Fred chose theirs. In Sandy's room was a small bed and mattress, and a few chairs piled in a corner. There was quite a lot of cleaning to be done, the curtains needed replacing, and most of the windows had damaged hinges or catches. Some of the panes of glass were cracked or missing. All of the woodwork needed a lick of paint, and some of it was damaged and in need of renewal.

When the family all met again downstairs, the boys heard from their parents that the house would need to be cleaned from top to bottom and all of the curtains thrown out and replaced. Their father told them that the roof, windows and some of the woodwork – including the flooring – was in desperate need of repair. Joe, who had helped him in the joiner's shop from time to time, would have to give him a hand. It would all take several months to complete.

They assembled again in the yard, and after John had locked the front door they all climbed onto the wagon. At that point they heard two dogs barking in a building nearby, whose door had a hole in one of its panels. It was out of this hole that the head of a young black dog popped out. It soon found itself pushed aside, as the head of an old brown dog with whiskers surged out, and that in its turn was displaced by the first dog – and so it went on. To the family it seemed like a Punch and Judy show. These antics continued for about a minute, making everyone roar with laughter.

The noise attracted one of the farm hands in the field, who ran up to the yard and shouted at the dogs to be quiet. They settled down finally, but only after a further madcap display through the hole in the door. The hand introduced himself as Jim Pollard – in fact he was senior farm hand – who said the dogs were his. It was his habit to leave them in the outbuilding while he was working. He asked if they were the new owners of the farm, to which John replied that they were. They weren't moving in, he said, until all the cleaning and major repairs were done. 'Yes, I remember you,' Jim Pollard said, talking to John. 'I remember you as a boy, playing here when your grandparents were alive and running the place.' He went on to outline one or two details concerning the farm and its stock, and said that Tremain, as a temporary arrangement through the bank, had been paying the farm hands' wages.

The family, after taking a last look at the farm, drove off.

Although Sandy and his brothers were excited about living

on a farm, their parents were slightly less enthusiastic, given the tasks that lay ahead. John's principal fear was that with so many roof slates either missing or damaged, the joists would suffer come the autumn rains. He couldn't help remarking that the farmhouse had been in excellent condition when his grandparents lived there.

Repair of the farmhouse

FOR THE next two weeks, and mainly at weekends, the family set about cleaning the farmhouse top to bottom. They threw out old carpets, curtains, clothes, papers, then thoroughly washed the floors and windows. John repaired some of the roof timbers and fitted new slates. Then he scooped out the moss and dirt from the gutters and drainpipes, one of which had to be replaced, as it was broken and leaked water over the windows and sills. Sandy's mother made and fitted new curtains, while the boys laid out the new carpets and arranged some of the furnishings.

John's next task, with the help of his eldest son Joe, was to repair the broken windows and replace some of the woodwork where damaged. All in all, it took about three months to make the place habitable. The final repair job was to the roof of one of the outbuildings, together with its wooden doors. Thereafter it was decided not to move into the farmhouse until the start of the school holiday, so as not to disrupt Sandy's education before he sat his entrance exam for grammar school.

They needn't have worried. Although Sandy had helped with the farmhouse, it didn't affect his school work, and he passed his exam. As the end of term approached, and he looked forward, Sandy began to relish the prospect of linking up with Tom and Jim again – though they of course would always be in the class above him.

Sandy's father assesses the future development of the farm

JOHN TOYE now began to look at the business of running the farm. He needed to determine what was required to replenish the stock, feed and seed for the next year, and so talked to Tremain, from whom he felt he could get sufficient information to gauge what sums of money were involved and the changes required.

To this end John sold his joinery business and house in Falmouth, with the money realised sufficient to give him the leeway he required. He could now make the farm fully productive over the coming year, and could afford to pay his farm hands.

The Toye family moves to the farmhouse

IT WAS just after the start of the school holidays that Sandy's father made arrangements for them to move. They used the wagon and trailer to transport the heavy furniture (most of the lighter furniture and some of the bedding having been taken to the farmhouse already). It took several trips to get it all done, and once the final load was tied down in the trailer they took a last look around the house in Falmouth. It was a sad day leaving the place they had so much come to love over the years.

The family quickly settled into their new home, with the boys pleased in particular, because they'd got their own rooms.

Previously they'd had to share. For their mother and father it was a joy to breathe the pleasant country air and to look forward to a life running their own farm. A routine quickly established itself, the boys all given tasks to do around the place. Sandy's job was to deliver milk to the surrounding cottages, houses and farms that didn't produce their own.

Sandy meets Margery Richards

AFTER ABOUT a week Sandy was asked to deliver milk to the Richards' farm. He went about his other deliveries as fast as he could, eager to announce to Tom that he was now living close by. He knocked at the farmhouse door. A young dark-haired girl of about the same age as himself answered. She didn't recognise him, despite previous visits here with his father. He asked whether Tom was about. Tom was out in one of the barns, she told him. She introduced herself, and likewise he explained who he was and where he lived. Margery said she knew that Benjamin Toye had died, and that his nephew John had been left the farm, and that John was a family man.

She led him to one of the barns above the farmhouse and shouted for her brother. Tom came out, pleased and surprised to see his old school friend. He told Margery all about their exploits. The two boys chattered about all the things they could do together, though in due course Sandy had to go back to the farm and continue his milk round. Before he left all three of them arranged to go for a swim on Sunday, though Tom and Margery would have to ask their parents first.

Sandy went back to the dairy and sorted out his other deliveries. Then he went inside to see his mother. As she was not too busy he was able to tell her about Tom and Margery. She said she knew that Tom had been a friend at school, but she didn't know Margery — that was a new name for her. He asked if he could go swimming on Sunday, and as he had been so helpful with the cleaning and other jobs she granted him permission. If the Richards' children were allowed also, she would make up a picnic basket for all of them.

Margery and Tom visit to the Toyes' new home

LATER THAT evening, after the Toye family had finished their meal, and retired to the parlour, there was a knock at the door. It was Margery and Tom. They were invited in to meet the family. John said he remembered them from the times when he did his joinery work at their farm. He asked them to pass on his family's regards to their parents. Once he'd finished repairing the farmhouse and outbuildings he would like to pay them a visit.

Sandy's mother showed Margery and Tom over the farmhouse, so that they could see what changes had been made. Margery said they had always been curious about the house and what it was like inside. She added that her parents had not been on friendly terms with Benjamin, as he was always making complaints about trivial problems, mostly caused by sheep straying from their own farm. Old Benjamin kept himself to himself and wasn't too open to people visiting his farm. The only person he tolerated was a woman who did his cooking and cleaning.

On their way out Sandy suggested that they walk with them as far as the northern end of Polwheveral Creek, where he had already been for a swim, and where they could all go on Sunday.

The other two were happy with this, and thought when they saw it that it seemed a safe place. Sandy would meet them at the entrance to their farm at nine o'clock on Sunday morning.

Visit to the creek

COME SUNDAY morning, Sandy rose early and after a hurried breakfast finished his chores with much the same haste. Sure enough, when he got to the Richards' farm, Tom and Margery were waiting. They had with them some food and drink to add to the picnic basket.

The weather was cool. Just before the creek there was a headland that they had to traverse before climbing down to the beach. To the three friends looking down it seemed like paradise, with the sun skipping on the water and the golden sand untouched by any other being. The creek was even hidden from view to any stray boat on the Helford Passage.

They climbed down to the sand and chose a place to lay out their mats, clothes and the picnic basket. Margery changed at the cliff-side, while the two boys put on their swimsuits there and then and ran into the water – which, being shallow, was really quite warm. Margery followed soon after.

As all three of them were able swimmers they enjoyed themselves thoroughly there in the sheltered water. They would dive off rocks – the water itself a dapple of sunlight – and once submerged would see a host of small fish swimming about. It was all such fun, especially for Sandy, who was so glad to get away from the drudgery of farm work.

When they were tired with swimming they waded to the sandy beach and dried themselves. They put all their mats together and opened the picnic basket. By now they were hungry, so pretty soon all the food was eaten. Having had their fill, they lazed on the beach and chatted. When, after about an hour, they were ready for another swim, they struck out into deeper water, where they dived for shells. All too soon it was time to pack up their clothes and put their rubbish in the basket and make their way back to the Richards' farm.

When Sandy had seen them home, he suggested another swim for next Sunday – perhaps this time with Jim Earle too. Tom said he'd be seeing Jim during the week, and so would ask.

Second visit to the creek, with Jim

WHEN SANDY made his visit to the Richards' farm on the following Sunday, there was Jim Earle waiting for him. He had come with his pony and cart. Sandy asked him how he liked living at Mawnan Smith. Jim really enjoyed it, he said, as in the country you were well away from the smoke and dust of the mines and factories. His father had even allowed him the use of a small rowing boat, for fishing trips in the Helford River.

Tom and Margery joined them, Margery remarking immediately that the pony and cart would save them so much time in getting to the creek. Indeed, it took Jim a very short while to drive them there, though they did have to walk along the headland. On climbing down, the four friends found as before that the beach was free of any other visitors. Soon they were in their costumes, splashing about and swimming.

Jim built a fire in a corner under the cliff and cooked some fish that he'd brought, which with the rest of the picnic proved quite a feast. After it, they certainly had to pause before another swim, and decided to explore the cliff. They were disappointed not to find any caves.

It was late in the afternoon when they climbed back up the cliff and walked down to the road where the pony was tethered. When, presently, they reached the Richards' farm, Jim said he had enjoyed it all so much that he wanted to invite them out in his rowing boat. 'How about next Sunday?' he said. His boat was berthed at Helford Passage, which was a long way for them, and so he agreed to collect them.

A trip to a cove in Jim's boat

SO TO next Sunday, and Helford Passage. When they arrived at the berth Jim collected the oars and they all climbed aboard. After casting off Jim rowed out into the river. He knew an ideal place – Perran Cove – little more than a mile away, where they could swim and have their picnic. They all agreed, and Jim set off.

Once there, and with the boat tied up, they changed, then gently eased themselves into the warm shallow water. Further out they could dive, where there were crabs crawling along the bottom. Later, Jim suggested catching shrimps, and pointed out some rock pools. He got some tins from the boat, and all four of them set about baling out the water in the pools, which then made it an easy job, scooping out the shrimps. When they'd got enough together Jim prepared a fire and cooked them, and so once again he had supplemented their picnic. Afterwards they explored the area all around the cove, Margery finding some unusual shells, which she put in her bag.

By the time they decided to tidy up and row the boat back to its berth, the tide was going out, so the boys had to haul it down the beach before they could all climb on board. They took it in turns to row. When the boat was safely berthed, Jim collected the pony and cart and drove from the field to the road where his friends were waiting. Back at the Richards' place, before going their separate ways, they arranged for another trip to Helford Passage the following week.

Visit to an island

WHEN THEY went out the following Sunday, Jim said he knew of an island not far along the coast. After casting off they all took it in turns rowing, as today the wind was against them. When they got to the island they found a sandy beach and pulled the boat up well clear of the water. Then they went off to explore. They found a nice spot, and here decided to build themselves a shelter where they could eat their meal. They chose two tall flat rocks close together for the main walls, and made the roof by over-spanning them with driftwood, which they found all over the island. Inside, large pieces of flotsam were perfect for seats.

After all their hard work they were hot and dirty, and so went for a swim on the island's landward side. After chasing small fish and diving off some rocks they returned to the shelter. They had their meal and walked round the island again, by which time it was late afternoon. It was a long row back, so they gathered up their things and hauled the boat back to the water. They needn't have worried. Rowing back to Mawnan was easier than they thought, because now the wind was behind them, and they made good time.

For their next trip out Sandy suggested they visit the smugglers' caves on the coast at Falmouth. As it was a long way he said they should try and persuade his older brother Joe to come along too, as he was an experienced rower. Thing was, they would have to go on a Saturday, as by now he'd missed church two Sundays running.

Happily, Joe was keen to join in. He said the repair work at the farm was pretty much complete, and that his father was coping with the farm work. He felt he could be spared for one day surely. So, on the Saturday following, Jim arrived at the Richards' place with a horse and wagon, where his three friends were waiting, as well as Joe, who were surprised to see the wagon. Jim explained that the pony would struggle to pull a cart with five persons.

They all climbed up and off they trundled to Helford Passage. At the berth there was a larger boat tied up, because again Jim was thinking about the numbers involved. It was one he'd borrowed from his father. They got in and pushed off, and Joe and Jim being the strongest, they did most of the rowing.

The weather was calm and the stroke work relatively easy. When they reached the cliffs at Falmouth they all helped to pull the boat up onto the shingle. They surveyed the cliffs, where Sandy found an enormous cave that may have been used by smugglers. They all climbed up to have a look.

Jim lit some candles he'd brought with him, and led the way. Sheepishly, the others followed. Despite the flicker of their flames, it was still very dark, and the atmosphere was eerie. After twenty paces or so they were stunned by the noise of someone snoring. On creeping in a few more yards they discovered an old man sleeping on some straw. He was wearing heavy clothes that had obviously seen better days. His hair was white and unkempt, and he wore a black patch over one eye.

When they got closer he woke up suddenly and growled. Although this frightened them a little, they soon recovered and started talking to him. He said his name was Jack Pengelly, and that he was living rough in various places round Falmouth. Most of his life he had been a seaman, until he had injured his leg. This happened in a storm while he was pulling in hawsers on a fishing boat, just off the Cornish coast. Sandy asked him why he wore an eye-patch. The old man replied that he'd lost an eye during a voyage in a cargo ship, plying between Falmouth and Brittany. The capstan went out of control and a part of its machinery broke off and pierced his eye.

They realised that the old man, odd though he was, was harmless, so they were quite happy talking to him. Soon however he left them to walk into Falmouth. Eccentric as undoubtedly he was, they decided to give him a nickname. As he had lost an eye they imagined him as a pirate. For that reason they called him Blind Pew, after a character in *Treasure Island*.

After some further explorations they climbed down the cliff to the beach. There they had a makeshift meal from the food they'd brought with them. They spent a bit more time in some other small caves, then when the five of them felt they had seen enough they decided to return.

The row back was harder, because now Joe and Jim had the wind against them. By keeping close to the shore they managed to avoid the worst of it, however, and once they were back at Helford Passage they were already planning their next expedition.

Heavy rains

HEAVY RAINS over the next weekend prevented the four friends exploring new areas. Instead they walked to the old barn on the hill above the Richards' farm. Inside they sat on some straw and talked about their previous adventures. The most interesting was the visit to the Falmouth cliff caves. What had most impressed itself on all of them was the encounter with the old man, or Blind Pew as they'd called him. The topic then turned to what they all expected to be doing when they were older.

Sandy said he would like to go to sea in merchant ships or join the Royal Navy. Then he could visit foreign lands, such as China,

India or Japan. Tom wanted to train as a mining engineer and improve the safety aspect of that line of work. With experience he might possibly rise to 'captain' of a tin or copper mine. Margery said she would like to manage her own farm and breed cattle, though she didn't think this was possible as her parents' farm was not very productive at present. The only way for her to manage a farm in the future would be to rent one and gradually develop the stock.

Finally Jim declared he was going to start as a shipwright apprentice in two years' time. After that was complete he'd be given training in the office of a boat-building firm. If that was successful then in time he could work alongside his father in the boat-building business.

Sandy's first year at grammar school

IN THE autumn of 1888, Sandy started at Falmouth Grammar School. Originally the Falmouth Classical and Mathematical School, it had been established in 1824, and catered for boys only. For girls entering higher education there were other schools. Margery for example went to the Falmouth County High School, which was at the corner of Cambridge Place and Albany Road.

Sandy's class was attended by about thirty boys. The subjects he had to study were English, mathematics, geography, history and elementary science. There was religious instruction also. He was surprised when they gave him a notebook and ink pen, the latter consisting a wooden stem and steel nib. At his previous school, work was mainly done on slates.

His teachers were strict but fair, so he settled in quickly and adapted to their routine. Throughout the year he did fairly well at most subjects, except English. He didn't seem to have any aptitude at all for this. His best work was in maths and geography, especially the latter (interested as he was in visiting foreign countries). The classroom was organised in rows of heavy double desks of oak, the type with a lid. Carved into many of these were the initials of previous pupils, some of whose names he could guess. Each desk had an inkwell with a brass cover, evidently much used in the past, as the surrounding wood was permanently stained.

At the front of the class and to one side was the teacher's high oak desk and stool. From this vantage he could see clearly whether his pupils were misbehaving or engrossed in their studies. On the wall behind the desk was a bamboo cane, long with a curved handle. That was used to punish boys who misbehaved. Although, as Sandy found out, the cane was rarely used, it did act as a powerful deterrent: bad behaviour didn't much occur in class.

Once again Sandy linked up with his friends Tom and Jim, though mainly at meal breaks, given their different classes. With Jim living some way from school, he was usually collected by his father with his horse and trap, on his way home from business. Tom and Sandy, living nearer to Falmouth than Jim, walked the two miles between home and school. Sometimes, when the weather was bad, they were picked up by one of the parents from either of the two farms.

Most days at meal breaks the three friends would wander round Falmouth, where they saw the different types of work going on in the factories or in the blacksmith's shop near to school. As the weeks went by they got bored with this, seeing the same old things day after day. As a remedy, Tom suggested one lunch-time that they visit his sister Margery, not far away at the County High School (which had only opened the previous year). To get there meant a walk down Trelawney Road into Florence Terrace, then the short distance along Cambridge Place, which was where the school was, at the corner of Albany Road.

When they got there all the girls were in the playground, playing hopscotch, or skipping, or busy with other games. After looking out carefully, Tom at last saw his sister walking round the corner of a building. He waved. She saw them and came over. She chatted through the railings, mainly to Tom, while Sandy and Jim ogled at all the other girls. They'd been there just a very short time when the school mistress, who'd been watching, came out, scolded them and chased them away. They ran up Cambridge Place and walked the rest of the way back to their own school, laughing at what had happened, but a little scared of the mistress nevertheless.

Other than meal breaks at school or the odd evening, the friends met up mainly at the weekends, as all of them had work to do when they got home from school. Jim had to help his father with his boat repair. Margery and Tom had things to do around the farm. Sandy had to make his milk deliveries on most evenings and early on Saturday mornings.

Preparation for their first winter at the farm

DURING THE autumn months the four friends visited the creek at Perran Cove for picnics, where as before they swam in the shallow water. The sea was warmest in August and September, so they were able to stay in for much longer periods. In October the weather was colder, so as an alternative the quartet met mainly at the old barn and planned what they would like to do during the coming year.

With winter approaching they met less frequently. There were other reasons besides the weather, one being that Jim had to help his father with his boat-building repair, two of his father's employees having been taken ill. For their part, Sandy, Margery and Tom were expected to take on more farm work in preparation for winter. Sandy and his brother also had to help with fetching and carrying for their father, who was now repairing the roofs and timbers in the outbuildings. It was expected that they would help too with tying down the haystacks against the winter winds. Sandy's older brother Joe had also to help his father repair the farm roads. This was done by filling in the dips and craters where the roads were liable to flooding. With the heavy winter rains many of the farm roads suffered such damage, so this was the kind of repair that was always essential. On top of that, when there were heavy snowfalls, the resulting drifts often made the roads impassable.

Winter feed and straw for bedding the farm animals had to be collected and heaved into the barns. Potatoes needed lifting from the fields and stored in the open, then given a covering of straw and earth to protect them from the frosts. Other vegetables had also to be harvested and stored.

In the kitchen the brothers had to help their mother with the kind of provisions that could be stored for use during the winter months. Onions and other vegetables were pickled in vinegar, boiled eggs were shelled and stored in 'water glass' or sodium silicate. Hams and fish were cured and hung in the cool cupboard. Butter and cheeses would be made and stored there also. All this was essential if the family wanted to last through the winter, especially if that proved to be long and cold.

Despite this flurry of activity, there were several interesting events taking place during the autumn and winter.

Halloween party

THE FIRST of these was when Sandy and his brothers were invited to the Richards' for a Halloween party. They had to dress up as ghosts or other weird characters. Sandy's mother prepared the costumes, Sandy and Joe going as pirates, while Fred was a ghost.

When they got to the party Mrs Richards took them into the kitchen, where on the floor was a tin bath full of water with small apples floating on the surface. In a corner of the room a cord was strung on to two hooks, and suspended from this were sticky buns. On a low cupboard was a pumpkin with its pith removed and a face cut into its shell. A candle glowed ghoulishly inside.

Margery and Tom were waiting for them, she dressed as a witch with a black cloak and pointed hat, and he as a skeleton with bones outlined on paper and sewn to his costume. On his head he wore a hood with slits for the eyes and mouth.

After they had all had drinks, the fun started – first off ducking for the apples in the bath. Everyone managed to lift at least one apple between their teeth, though without exception all got soaked in water – Margery especially. Once dried out and rubbed down with towels, it was on to the next game. This time each one in turn had to kneel on a chair and hold the handle end of a fork in their teeth, then drop it in the bath so that it skewered one of the apples – which, as in the previous game, they were allowed to eat. Most managed to get the fork through an apple, but Tom – no matter how many times he tried – simply couldn't do it, even though there were a great many apples left.

Next was the game with the sticky buns. Each one in turn had to sit in a chair placed by one of the buns on a string, which was covered in treacle. The player was blindfolded and had to keep hands behind his or her back – and when the bun was set swinging had to take a bite. After several goes the children got the hang of it, though not without getting covered in treacle, necessitating many a face-wash.

When the games were over Mrs Richards brought out sweets and cakes, then as the hour advanced it was time to wind things up and send everyone home. The three Toye brothers thanked her so much and made their way out into the night.

'Robins alight'

ONE NIGHT at the end of November, when Sandy called on Margery and Tom, he found them near the old barn by an open fire cooking potatoes. Shortly after that the sound of a cart approaching from below the farm announced that Jim too was on his way here. He shouted out their names, and in the darkness they called back, guiding him to where they were.

Presently Jim joined them by the fire, now a merry blaze, what with the dry branches from an old oak that Margery and Tom had gathered. They gave him a cooked potato, which although it looked black and charred was still deliciously edible once peeled. They all tucked in. Their feast over, Jim suggested a game of 'robins alight', which the others asked him to explain. What you had to do was pass a lighted stick from one to another, and the person holding it when the flame went out had to pay a forfeit.

They all agreed to join in the game, and soon had the burning stick passing from one to another, eager hands twisting it this way and that in order to keep it alight. Presently the stick came to Margery and the flame went out. The boys all shouted, 'Forfeit for you!'

Margery, not quite knowing what the boys would ask as a forfeit, waited with bated breath. Jim was first to speak – what she had to do, he said, was go down to the Toyes' farm, milk a cow in the dark and bring it back for the boys to drink. Up she jumped immediately, setting off at a jog to the farm, where she picked up a small churn. She crept over to the stalls where the cows were under cover for the night, finding her way in none too easily, given that it was pitch black inside. Luckily the cow she lit on was one of the docile ones, and she was able to milk it till the churn was full. She climbed the hill again, and triumphantly produced her forfeit.

The four friends sat round the fire and passed the burning stick once more – and this time it fell to Jim. His forfeit, the others decided, was to hop on one leg while tapping the top of his head with one hand and drawing a circle with the other. He had to keep this up for a count of a hundred. He just about managed it to fifty, but then lost his balance and co-ordination, and fell over in a heap. The others roared with laughter.

Next forfeit was Sandy's, and for his turn he had to walk blindfold for the length of a fallen tree trunk. He started well, but soon ran in to trouble in a tangle of branches, which much impeded his progress. The others hooted at him for being so slow, but after a few near trips he did complete the forfeit, to the cheers and delight of them all.

One final forfeit would be the most difficult. Another lighted stick was drawn from the fire, and this time was passed around very fast. Tom didn't quite work out that the other three had quietly agreed that the last and most difficult task should fall to him, and indeed when the flame went out it was he who was left with the smoking stick. Jim, a broad smile spreading across his face, explained to Tom that what he had to do was walk to the cottage high on the hill above the farm, in the shelter of some gnarled old trees. An old lady lived there, who always dressed in black, and had a cat with strange, staring, darting eyes. Villagers kept their distance, as weird goings-on were reputed to happen here. Tom had to walk round the cottage perimeter three times. When he set off, the others followed at a distance.

He did his three circuits as noiselessly as possible, but just at the point where he was completing his forfeit, the old lady's cat, until now cowed in the undergrowth, spat and snarled at him and rushed out into the open. Tom turned in panic and fled down the hill, as did the others, who were not only not far behind but were more frightened than he. When they reached the fire they were all of them a-tremble, with fright and laughter combined. For Tom's bravery, he was given a hearty cheer.

It was late now and they'd all had excitement enough for one day, and making their way home wondered if their dreams would be haunted by the black cat with staring eyes.

Margery loses her cat

ONE EVENING in December, when he'd finished cleaning the outbuildings where the pigs and hens were kept, Sandy went up to the Richards' farm. When he got there Margery told him she'd lost her cat. She was so upset by this that Tom and Sandy began to look around. They searched the barns and sheds, but nowhere could the cat be found. Next they began to look lower down, in the southern part of the farm – but no luck there either. However, in the course of these wanderings, Sandy came to an old and disused cottage, home to one of the farm workers many years before. Having looked around inside he came out and saw Tom near a well not far from the cottage garden. The well had had its cover partly removed. Both could hear faint cries and mewing coming from inside. They pulled the cover off completely, and peering down could see the cat crouching at the bottom, unhurt (with one of its nine lives, it had landed not in water but on a bed of dry mud).

Tom ran back to the farmhouse and fetched a long rope. This he secured to the iron pillar from which you lowered the bucket, and played it out, down into the depths. As Sandy was the smaller of the two and more nimble than Tom, it was he who climbed down. The well's interior was of rough local stone, and offered many projecting footholds. The cat when he reached it was frightened of course, and so had to be coaxed. Eventually all was well, for when Tom sent down on the rope an old bucket he found, the cat was cradled and hoisted to safety. When Sandy climbed up after, they pushed the cover back into position.

They returned to the farmhouse, where Margery was overjoyed. To be sure that the cat didn't wander off and cause another incident, it was shut up in a room for the night.

Winter at the farm

IT WAS now the end of December, 1888, and after the Christmas celebrations the weather turned much colder, with high winds and heavy rain. Outside of school hours, Sandy and his brothers were confined to the farmhouse most evenings.

They amused themselves with card games and painting. The youngest brother, Fred, entertained himself with the wooden blocks and shapes his father had made for him. Occasionally Sandy's father would play cribbage with the oldest brother Joe. On rare occasions he brought out a set of wooden skittles, which the family would play with in the hall. Joe and Sandy became quite skilled. Fred, much younger as he was, didn't have the strength to throw the wooden balls effectively.

If the winter winds abated, sometimes Sandy's parents would hitch up the horse and wagon and take the three brothers to Falmouth. There they would wander round the harbour, or simply watch the spume crashing on the distant rocks. If they went on a Saturday, large ships were sometimes berthed, and Sandy would watch for hours as cranes unloaded their cargo. Such trips always ended in a cold ride home on the wagon, so on their return Sandy's mother prepared hot drinks for all, and a meal she had partly prepared before they'd set off.

Sometimes the brothers had to dress up in their best clothes and be taken to have tea with two old aunts. Although they didn't like the dressing-up bit, the brothers enjoyed these visits, as they were always given sweets.

Spring arrives, 1889

WITH AN end to the severe weather, and the arrival of spring, new pleasures were visited on the Toye family. Activities around the farm abounded. The first priority was clearing away the debris that had collected round the outbuildings under the force of the winter storms. Fallen branches were collected and sawn into logs. Feed and bedding for the farm animals had to be replenished, and repairs to the barn roofs were again necessary. A start was made on preparing the fields for growing vegetables and other crops. Next the ploughs were brought out and checked. As some were worn they were taken to the local blacksmith for minor repairs. At the same time Sandy's mother went off to Falmouth with the horse and wagon to buy provisions to renew her dwindling kitchen stocks.

So for Sandy the early part of spring was a busy time, with much to do. Sometimes he saw Margery and Tom, when he delivered the milk, but for the next two weeks Sandy had little time to see his friends.

Sandy's father found it an exceptionally busy time, especially as this was his first spring at the farm. One important task that he had to get out of the way was the removal of a large uprooted tree that was partially blocking one of the roads. He took his farm hands and the two best horses to help. Once at the scene he looped the ropes he'd brought with him round the girth of the tree and tied the free ends to the horses' harnesses. At first when the horses pulled, the tree didn't budge. Then one of the farm hands sawed away at the roots, which were still embedded in the ground.

This time the ropes gradually pulled the tree away from where it had fallen. They hauled it down the road and through a gate to the nearest field. There the farm hands stripped and sawed off the branches, then with a crosscut saw sliced the trunk into several large logs. With that job done, they loaded up the wagon and brought their timber back to the farm.

In the evening Sandy and Joe helped unload. They had to stack the large logs with smaller pieces in between, to allow in the air to circulate, so keeping their timber dry.

The friends go to young Billy's aid

AS THE farm work eased off briefly the four friends met again at the old barn. Margery had a problem that she wanted the lads to solve. Young Billy Venning, who did casual work about the place, was being bullied by a certain group of youths. This always happened on his return home from work to where he lived in Constantine. She said that Billy was a cripple, having had one of his legs crushed in a mining accident. He walked with the aid of a crutch. It meant he had an awkward gait, which some of the local youth couldn't help making fun of. Fortunately for Billy, he was friendly with the senior farm hand, who happened to live at Ponjeravah, which was near Constantine, to whose outskirts he would take him each evening. Thereafter Billy was alone.

Quite often, as he walked along Constantine's Main Street, these same youths would be waiting for him, all ready with their taunts. As time went on, these grew worse and worse. On Saturday last, the four waiting for him were standing in a line barring his path. This time when they taunted they also pulled at his clothes.

Worse was to come. One of them kicked his crutch away. Billy staggered and fell to the ground. Once down he was sworn at and kicked. Then, luckily this time, a man coming out of a nearby house chased his assailants away.

Jim said that he visited Constantine sometimes and had heard about these youths. He was all for them helping Billy with his problem. They would need to match the gang of four with the same number themselves, so Sandy would have to ask his brother Joe to help. Margery said that the problem was at its worst on a Saturday, when the gang had been drinking cider.

Joe agreed to the plan, which on the following Saturday saw Jim take them all to Constantine before Billy was driven home. They went with his pony and cart, which they left in a field just outside Constantine. They secreted themselves in a side street adjacent to Main Street, and waited for what seemed an age. In due course the four local bullies arrived on the scene and took up their positions in readiness for Billy, who, when he appeared, was subjected to the usual hostilities.

Jim, who was watching from the corner, signalled the others to follow him out and confront the youths, all of whom, as Margery had predicted, were full of drink. The four lads advanced towards them expecting to scare them off. Instead they turned on them and started to fight. Joe, being the strongest, took on the biggest, who seemed to be their leader. Sandy, Tom and Jim lined themselves up against the other three. After trading punches Sandy was knocked to the ground, but got up instantly, and matched the other blow for blow. Tom and Jim also gave as good as they got, though much of the time had to resist being dragged to the ground.

Joe, always handy with his fists, was getting the better of the leader. When the latter stopped for breath he grabbed him round the neck and swung him off his feet. Then he dragged him to the side of the road and ducked his head in a horse trough. After several more dips the youth struggled free and ran away up the road. The others, seeing their leader in retreat, soon freed themselves and ran after him. Joe and the others shouted after them, to the effect that they'd get much worse if they ever attacked Billy again.

When the four bullies were far enough away, Joe and the others chatted with Billy for a few minutes, then returned to the field with their pony and cart, from where Jim drove them back to the Richards' place. Margery was there waiting, and after hearing their story thought they were very brave.

When Sandy and Joe got home, and went into the parlour, their parents were horrified, the two boys being in such a state. Both were bruised badly about the face, with their clothes torn and spattered with dirt. Not unnaturally, their father gave them a telling off. He calmed down a little when they told him about Billy, and why they had confronted the bullies.

The following night Mr and Mrs Richards came over to see Sandy's parents, to talk about what had happened. The four adults could agree that while they couldn't condone the boys' behaviour, they did admire them for springing to Billy's aid. Later, when Sandy and Joe were summoned to the parlour, Mr and Mrs Richards couldn't help laughing at the boys, as each of them had a beautiful black eye.

They revisit the creek

THE FOUR friends met again at the barn one week after the fight. The black eyes had disappeared, and now there were only swellings under the eyes. Jim and Tom had likewise been told off by their parents, but had been commended for their motive nevertheless. Margery said that she had seen Billy during the week, and he'd told her he'd had no trouble since.

The only other outing the four friends had during that April was a visit to the creek for a picnic. Jim collected the others, as usual, at the Richards' farm, though this time everyone brought heavy coats, as the creek was exposed to the wind. They selected a spot under the cliff for protection.

At first the lads were reluctant to swim, and it took all Margery's wiles to goad them into the water. They didn't last long, it has to be said: the water was so icy cold it turned them blue and made them shiver. Jim lit a fire, and having warmed up they got dressed and had their picnic.

Tom had brought a fishing line and bait, and set himself up beyond the beach by the rocks. From there he cast his line repeatedly, without ever catching a fish. He gave up after about half an hour, and re-joined the others by the fire. Here Sandy was asking Jim what was the fishing boat his father had under repair at Falmouth. His own father had seen it on one of his visits into town. The craft was a forty-foot carvel-built boat. The port side had been badly damaged where she had been thrown on the rocks in a storm. Only its strong diagonal planking had stopped it sinking.

Margery strolled along the beach looking for different coloured seashells. They came in shades of red, brown and white, and there were also razor shells of a bluish hue. Those that took her eye she collected in a bag. She looked back at the boys sitting round the fire, and knew that over the next two to three weeks they would all be too busy to meet up again. Sandy had to help his father clear the fields for ploughing. Margery and Tom had work around the farm. Jim was needed by his father to help repair a fishing boat.

The ploughing competition

ON THE following Monday evening Sandy and Joe were told that they had to start clearing the fields. Their father took them in the wagon to the first of these that had to be ploughed. There were huge stones that had to be removed and loaded into the wagon. So soon as they had dealt with the top half of the field, Jim Pollard started to plough. The plough he used had a skim coulter: its movement just behind the disc threw up the top crop remains, which it pared off into the bottom of the furrows. Sandy was amazed to see how easily the plough did this, while leaving fresh soil on top.

When they had finished clearing the first field, they moved on to the next. After about an hour of that it was getting late and was time to stop. After loading the stones in the wagon their father drove them back to the farmhouse for supper.

The next evening Sandy, Joe and their father finished what they'd started, though towards evening discovered that at the lower end of the field the ground was waterlogged. It was found that the tiles forming the drainage channel had fallen in and that stones and soil were blocking the channel. The three of them cleared the blockage as best they could, and next evening replaced the tiles. When they had done that John went to see how the ploughing was coming along. By now Jim had finished the top field and was part way down the lower, and making good progress. His boss complimented him on the progress he'd made.

What impressed John the most was how straight the furrows were. This gave Jim the opportunity to ask his employer if he would allow him to enter a ploughing competition, which was being held at a farm near Truro in just over two weeks' time. He said that at first he'd been reluctant to ask, because his previous employer – John Toye's uncle – had always refused. John was a different proposition however, and did not hesitate to let him enter. He was sure they could make it a day out for both families, and said he would supply the wagons for transport, as well as the ploughing equipment. Jim thanked him profusely, adding that the ploughing here at the farm would be finished well before the competition.

John went back to the bottom of the field and helped his two sons collect the remaining stones and debris, which they loaded on the wagon. He drove them back to the farm, and after all the muddy work with the drainage channel they had to wash themselves down before going into the farmhouse. Elizabeth, when she saw them, demanded that they change their clothes, as the smell of drainage still permeated their attire, and was very unpleasant.

After supper, John told them about Jim and the ploughing competition. Would they all like to go? They were all enthusiastic, especially as there would be stalls and other amusements there. Mrs Toye said she would prepare a picnic basket, while John would lend one of his wagons to Jim. He also told his sons that they had to have all their jobs completed before the day came round – in particular there were two other fields that needed clearing.

At the weekend Sandy and Joe had to help their father drive the wagon piled with stones to one of the old farm roads. Their work there was where the roadway had sunk and needed building up. This wasn't the only place, as there was another part of the road where a similar repair was needed. They had numerous tasks also over the next two weeks, so they were very glad when the day of the ploughing competition arrived at last. Jim collected the wagon early and loaded up the equipment and harnessed the horses he was going to use. Then he returned home and collected his family.

While the Pollard family were on their way, the Toye family were making their preparations. Sandy had finished his milk deliveries, Joe had fed the hens, and their father was finishing a repair in one of the barns. Elizabeth meanwhile put together the picnic.

When John had finished his work he brought out their horse Blackie from the stable and hitched him up to the wagon, by which time the family were ready to go. They all climbed up and set off for Truro. Their journey took them through the villages of Mabe, Perranarworthal and Carnon Downs, on a day that was warm and still. When they arrived at the farm a group of competitors were ready with their horses and ploughs, and the stalls and amusements were already doing a brisk trade.

John tethered the horse while his wife took Joe, Sandy and Fred to sample the amusements – hoopla, skittles and a coconut shy. Joe won a coconut. Sandy, after several tries at knocking down the skittles, won a book. All three boys had a toffee apple and sweetmeats. Then they made their way back to the wagon. John had been to the competition area, and told them that Jim had got second place with his ploughing. The farm hand who won had been coming to competitions for many years and was an excellent ploughman.

They all went over to see Jim and his family. Jim was congratulated on his success, and the two families began to get acquainted. Later, Sandy helped his mother spread out a cloth and set out the picnic. There was plenty to eat and the boys were soon tucking in – with the apple tarts and cream buns voted the best. It was then that they couldn't help but burst into laughter at little Fred with cream all over his face and jam in his ears. He'd *certainly* enjoyed himself.

The boys helped their mother tidy up while John gave the horse some feed and water. Then they drove home. It had been a successful outing, and the more John thought about it the more he felt inclined to enter his head farm hand for the ploughing competition next year.

Preparation for spring sowing

AT THE end of ploughing at the Toyes' farm – a week after the competition – John met with his senior hand to discuss business. John wanted to talk about his crops, and was particularly interested in matters of timing. Jim was so much more experienced here, and so it was left to him to comment on what to sow in the various fields. He suggested that for those on the top of the hill they grow mangels, for feeding the cattle. Here the soil was heavy and not suitable for cereals. In the lower fields they should plant seed for growing oats and barley. Broadly John agreed, but said he also wanted to grow wheat in one of the lower fields. The very lowest was the most sheltered, being under the hill and south-facing. Jim didn't disagree, and added that the field was well drained and had good soil. He recalled that Benjamin Toye *hadn't* grown wheat, as other farms had had failures in the past. Despite that, to Jim it was worth the risk – especially as recently wheat had got a good price at market.

There was one drawback, he said. Harvesting the wheat would require a number of sickles or reap hooks. Having grown just oats and barley in the past, the farm had nothing other than scythes for harvesting those crops. Wheat stalks were firm, and needed sickles, and on that understanding John agreed to their purchase.

Although he partly knew the answer, he asked Jim whether Benjamin Toye had ever considered modern harvesting equipment. Jim had to tell him that his uncle had always been tight with his money and rarely took the risk of buying anything he felt would not give a good return on his investment. To him modern contraptions, for example the mechanical harvester, were more suited to large farms – and as far as he was concerned that was the end of the matter.

Each year Benjamin had hired in extra hands to cut the barley and oat crops, and John would have to do the same – the most experienced hands being needed for harvesting during August or September. When John next took his horse and wagon and drove to the market at Falmouth – to buy seed, sickles and other tools – he took the time to chat with other farmers that he met. On his way home he collected Sandy from school – much to the latter's surprise, as he usually had to walk. Sandy told him all about the work he'd done in class, but then looked in the back of the wagon and suddenly stopped. Seeing the seed and hoes, he had a good idea what it all meant. However, the cutting tools with large broad blades and knobs at the ends of the handles he did not recognise. His father explained that these were sickles. This year he intended to grow wheat in one of the fields, and as the stalks would be tougher than those of barley or oats, the scythes they had at the farm wouldn't be up to the job. The hook shape was designed to allow the blade to cut more easily.

They were soon home. Sandy jumped down and opened the door of the barn where his father stored the tools. He gave him a hand to unload, and when they had finished stowing it all away they disappeared into the farmhouse. After washing, they went into the parlour to see the rest of the family before their evening meal.

A visit to the boat slip at Porth Navas

ABOUT A fortnight after the ploughing competition, Sandy called at the Richards' farm, on a Saturday afternoon. Tom told him they were still busy, but would see him later that evening at the barn. Tom had had a visit from Jim Earle during the week, and they'd agreed to meet after the evening meal. Sandy went back home and got on with his milk deliveries.

After supper he went to the old barn, where he met Jim, Margery and Tom. They all settled down in the straw and Sandy told them about the trip to Truro, and how Jim Pollard had won himself second prize. The others talked about what they had been doing. For Margery and Tom, it had all been farm work, and they were really in need of a break. Jim said that he'd got a suggestion for a Sunday outing. His father had finished repairs to the fishing boat at Porth Navas, and it was being floated off the slip at high tide on Monday morning. Would they like him to collect them on Sunday afternoon with the pony and cart and take them to see the boat before it went? An unqualified yes was the answer.

When Sunday came, and they were on their way – the horse climbing the hill to the boat slip – they could see the boat some way in the distance. To them it looked as if it floated on the air without support. As they drew closer they could see the trolley system underneath, with wooden shores propping the hull at equal intervals along its length.

Jim drove on and tethered the pony close to the workshop above the slip. When his three friends climbed out they got a good look at the boat. It was as good as new, with freshly applied blue and white paint, and the port registration sign gleaming in the sunshine. As the four climbed the ladder to the deck Jim's father appeared from below and asked them how they liked the boat. Sandy, Tom and Margery said it was looking very good.

On deck they admired the polished brasswork, twinkling in the sun. Jim's father invited them into the cabin and said they could try the steering. He explained how it operated. Only Sandy and Tom did so, swinging the wheel to starboard and port. With it they could hear the chains clanking, as they controlled the rudder.

Mr Earle showed them round the rest of the boat, then invited them into the workshop, where he gave them some lemonade. He asked his visitors how their respective parents were faring, now that the long winter was past. All were well, busy with the spring planting. After chatting for a little longer he said he had to go back to the boat, to make some final checks.

Later that evening, after exploring the area, Jim collected the pony and cart and drove his three friends back to the Richards' place. There and then they all decided that as they were still very busy they wouldn't meet up again for several weeks, unless something really interesting came up.

By the middle of May most of the urgent work around the farm was complete, so Sandy and Joe had more opportunities for other activities. Sandy still had his milk deliveries to do, but even so that gave him plenty of spare time at weekends.

Sandy meets the gardener of the Bonallack mansion

WITH LITTLE to do on the following Saturday Sandy was cleaning the courtyard at the rear of the farmhouse when his mother shouted to him from the kitchen. She wanted him to run an errand. It was to deliver a churn of milk to the cook at the

Bonallack mansion house. He took the churn and heaved it on to the cart, then he led the horse from the stable and put on its harness, bit and reins. Finally he hitched the horse to the cart and drove off to the mansion house.

When he got there the drive was long and curved. Part way up he stopped, amazed at what he saw happening on the lawn. The gardener was leading a horse that was pulling a wheeled device that was cutting the grass. It was a large appliance that had rotary blades, which cut the grass under power of the horse pulling it along. Sandy had never seen a mechanised grass cutter before. On the farms it was done with large scythes (for large areas) or with sickles (for borders or edges). For this part of Cornwall, the horse-drawn cutter was nothing short of an innovation.

The gardener knew the Toyes, and he called out to Sandy. If he was interested he could see the machine at close quarters, after he'd made his delivery. Sandy made haste with the churn, and back out on the front lawn was able to study the whole mechanism as the horse powered it along. After that the gardener showed him round the mansion grounds, which had a fair sprinkling of unusual plants and trees.

Flanking the house was a large garden set out with so wide a variety of flowers that there were many he couldn't recognise. Edging the garden was a low flat stone building with a small heavy door. The gardener explained that this was used to store ice for use in the kitchen. Beyond this was an area surrounded by high walls, where there were fruit trees in blossom – apple, pear, plum. In some instances, the branches had been trained along the walls.

Not far from there were strawberry and raspberry beds. There were also glass houses for lettuce, cucumber and tomato plants. On an upper level inside one of the greenhouses were grapevines hanging from above. At the rear of the house was another lawn with a sundial at its centre. Here he learned how you used it to tell the time of day. To the far side of the house was another lawn, this time with a pond. It had goldfish in it.

At the end of the tour – for that's what it was – Sandy thanked the gardener for sparing so much of his time. He was about to drive his horse and cart back to the farm when Mr Bonallack came out of the house and told him to wait. The gardener said he hoped he didn't mind that he had shown Sandy round. Mr Bonallack said that he didn't mind at all. He asked Sandy if his friends would like to see the gardens next Saturday at two in the afternoon. If so, he would also show them his telescope and photographic equipment. Sandy was sure his friends would jump at the chance.

He thanked him and drove off in the cart. He couldn't get back quick enough to tell his family, firstly about the amazing gardens, then about the grass cutter. He had to wait when he did arrive, because first he must stow the cart, then stable and feed and water the horse. When he went inside at last, the evening meal was under preparation. His mother asked him what had kept him so long – so now of course it all came gushing out: the gardener, the gardens he tended, Mr Bonallack, his telescope, the offer to his friends.

Everyone was eager to hear all about it, and not wishing to disappoint them Sandy went into all the detail. His father took him aside, and told him that when Sandy visited the mansion house again he must be on his best behaviour, and was sure that his friends' fathers would say exactly the same. It was a privilege for them to be invited.

The four friends visit the mansion house

THE NEXT day Sandy met up with his friends in the barn after church, and when they heard the news all were keen to make the visit. He told them all about the horse-drawn mower, though as to the sundial Jim said he already knew how it worked, as there was one on an estate near his home. However, they all met up again on the next Saturday and drove off to the mansion house. When they got there Mr Bonallack came out to greet them, having looked out for their pony and cart coming up the drive. He called the gardener over and got him to show them round. First stop was the walled garden with its plants and its fruit trees. Then came the grass-cutter, with a full demonstration out on the back lawn.

Next he showed them the beds with exotic flowers, which Margery found enchanting (for the sheer variety of colour). The other three weren't so interested and asked if they could look at the sundial. After several attempts, or several stray readings off the calibrated plate, the boys did eventually manage to tell the time. Lastly the gardener showed the four friends the icehouse, with its frozen blocks inside.

Finally he took them to the house, where they were met by Mr Bonallack, who led them into the main hall and up the long staircase. At the top was a playroom, with its door wide open. In a corner was a rocking horse, exquisitely painted, and next to that a playpen littered with toys. On the floor were some wooden blocks, all coloured differently and with numbers painted on. Against a wall was a doll's house, its rooms fitted with tiny furniture. There were also hoops and skipping ropes.

Mr Bonallack said his children were out with their mother, off visiting friends in Falmouth. He ushered them to a front-facing room that had large windows. There was a stand with a large telescope with a table and chairs positioned round it. On the table were several books on astronomy, which Mr Bonallack explained as the study of stars and planets. One by one they were allowed to look through the telescope, and were amazed at how clearly it showed them distant objects.

Mr Bonallack then led them to another room, which had a second one adjoining – the latter being completely without windows. This was where he kept his photographic equipment. It was, he said, his dark room, and here he developed his photographs. His young guests knew what photography was, but until now had no idea of how photographs were taken and developed. He took them inside, where they all had to take care, as here there were dishes filled with chemicals. He showed them how to develop negatives and the chemicals used in that process. All had to be done in darkness, he said, because light coming into the room would spoil the final result. To that end he pulled a black curtain across the door.

Later, he showed them photographs he had taken of his family, and of places round Falmouth, Penzance and other parts of Cornwall. This being an era where photography was still in its infancy, and not viable commercially, the four friends were naturally amazed at what they saw – at how lifelike all these pictures were. Their host only smiled, then finished off with a trip to the kitchen, where he told cook to give them lemonade and cakes. Mr Bonallack then escorted his guests to the main door and asked them how they'd enjoyed their day. Very much, was the unanimous reply – they were especially taken with the telescope and photography. They thanked him enormously for going to so much trouble. He waved after them once they were up on the cart and were meandering down the drive.

They build a rope bridge

IT WAS a fine day when they all met up again on the following Saturday. Sandy had got some old ropes, and suggested they might come in handy, exploring the woods north of Constantine – which to the others sounded a good idea. It took about half an hour to get there, and they soon found themselves a clearing where they could tether the pony.

The four friends pushed their way through the undergrowth and found a stream, overhung on either bank by trees – ideal for a rope bridge, a project they embarked on without delay. They stretched the heaviest rope across first, tying its ends to the trunks. Then came some of the smaller ropes – or guide ropes – which they tied higher up on the trees. These they lashed to the heavier main rope, spaced at three-foot intervals, to form a kind of hammock shape.

When they tried out their bridge they all, at the first attempt, slipped on the main rope and fell into the stream, getting their feet and legs wet – though after several more tries all mastered it. They could pretend that crossing the stream was like passing over a huge chasm, with a river in spate crashing and foaming beneath them. When they got tired of it they washed their feet and put their stockings and boots back on, which were damp. Then they made their way back to the clearing where the pony was tethered, which Jim fed and watered while the others spread out the picnic.

Come evening they were tired but happy, and trundled home weary and contented.

Visit to an old tin mine

THE MINE Tom really wanted to visit was the disused Killifrith tin mine, though the other three weren't that keen at first. He had to persuade them to go. They chose a Saturday and set off at about 8.30 in the morning. Jim drove them in the cart as usual, setting off in the direction of Deveron (as directed by Tom). To the others, this was the long way round, with Stithians and Gwennap a more obvious route. Tom explained that by going via Deveron they could see other mines and several factories on the way. Sure enough, once they had reached Deveron and crossed the Carnon river they could see the factories ahead. They took the road to Chasewater, following the Redruth and Chasewater railway. On the approach to Bissoe there was an arsenic works, with its tapering square stack belching smoke and sparks. That combined with the noise, it was easy to imagine a fiery dragon lurking somewhere nearby.

They continued their journey following the railway, passing through Twelveheads, on to Chasewater, then finally turning down to Killifrith, where there were both working and disused mines. When they got to the mine Tom was set on, they could almost feel the eerie presence of the generations of tinners who had worked there in the past. The only movement was the rustle of bushes and the creak of loose sheeting on the roof of an outbuilding. Tom, with his courage in his hands, began to walk around the ghostly buildings. Tentatively, the others followed.

The boiler stack and engine house were still in a good state. The mine had been closed down only in the last ten years, and there remained coal and tin ore lying around, as if a re-opening was expected any moment. Nor had so much time passed that there was a significant growth of weeds in the loading area close to the mine.

Their curiosity steadily overcoming their fear, they began to explore more of the outbuildings, where there were still some old rusty tools lying about. In one of the buildings was a damaged kibble, a device used to lift ore from the mine. In another were upturned boxes and benches, where the tinners took their food. They even found some old newspapers.

The four friends moved on to the main engine house, with its shaft and old workings. They decided to make believe that they were operating the mine. Tom worked the engine and whim for lifting out the ore. Sandy and Jim kept the boilers alive with coal.

Margery was a bal-maiden, and with a pointed hammer she happened to find, her job was cobbing the ore into smaller pieces. They kept it up for about an hour, until Margery was tired (not to say grey with the powder that came from the ore). Tom was dirty with oil from the engine, and Sandy and Jim were black with coal dust. To add to their woes, Sandy fell off the pile of coal and skinned his knees.

Margery looked at the others' dirty faces, their eyes ringed with white, and said they looked as if made up for Halloween. They all looked at one another and laughed. Tom said they couldn't go home in such a state, and what's more Sandy had to clean up the blood from his knees. Margery led them out to a stream nearby, and with cloths from the cart they managed to wash and make themselves presentable. Sandy's knees, after taking off the blood, weren't so bad after all.

For lunch they enjoyed the bread, cheese, fruit and milk that Margery had brought – the best they'd had in weeks, or so it seemed. When, later, it was a dirty and dishevelled band that had made its way home, Margery, Tom and Sandy jumped from the cart and slunk off for a good wash and change before being seen by their parents.

Haymaking

ONE DAY at the end of June Mr Richards called on John Toye, to ask if he could hire some of his hands to help cut hay for his animals' winter feed. As all John's planting was over, and his hands were mainly hoeing in the vegetable fields, he had no objections. They could start next Monday morning.

Sandy and his brother Joe overhead the conversation, and asked their father if *they* could help with the cutting. They wanted to learn more about haymaking. John said he would ask Mr

Richards about that the following day, which he did, with the result that his two sons would be welcome in the evenings, starting next Monday. The only proviso was that Joe, who had already left school and was working full-time on the farm, had to get his own farm work done first.

So, on the Monday, John Toye's farm hands turned up at the Richards' farm and started mowing the grass, using scythes, with Mr Richards pleased at the progress they made. By the time Sandy and Joe turned up, much of the grass had already been cut. Mr Richards thought about it for a moment, then gave them a pronged fork each and asked them to turn over the piles of cuttings in the upper field, to help it dry out. They set to and by the end of the evening, with help from the other hands, had turned over all the grass. The next evening they did much the same, only this time in the lower field. On this occasion though there was an accident. Robert Pascoe, one of the hands, cried out in pain, having stumbled and badly cut his calf with his scythe. Blood was seeping through the tear in his trouser leg. Mr Richards raced down the field, and with a knife cut away at the trousers. The wound was deep and the bleeding heavy.

Richards, afraid of excessive blood loss, took off his own belt and with it made a tourniquet to staunch the flow. Then he tore pieces from Robert's shirt to bandage the wound, which he secured with cord. He shouted out to Tom, who fetched the wagon, on to which the wounded young man was gently lifted, who by this time had fainted. They covered him with coats, then Richards hopped up on to the driver's seat and set off for the hospital in Falmouth. There they were received by a nurse and two porters, who lifted him onto a stretcher and took him to theatre. A doctor examined, cleaned up the wound, then arranged for the patient to be sedated. Once Robert Pascoe was asleep, the wound was stitched.

The doctor came out and found Tom and his father anxiously

waiting for news. He handed Mr Richards his trouser belt and said that by using it he'd certainly saved the young man's life. He explained that the severity of the wound had necessitated a very large number of stitches, and that the patient was still under sedation – though comfortably tucked up in bed. They'd have to keep him in for several days, because with so large a loss of blood it would take him some time to recover.

Mr Richards thanked the doctor for acting so promptly, and said he would pay the costs. After that, he drove to Robert Pascoe's parents, where Mrs Pascoe was already anxiously waiting, having heard about the accident from one of the hands. He told her about the operation and stitches, and above all that her son was comfortable. He arranged to take her and her husband to see him.

Next evening Sandy and Joe went up to the Richards' farm, and started work again. They had to rake the cuttings into piles then load them into the wagons, to be taken to where a hayrick was under construction. That same evening Richards drove his horse and trap to the Pascoes', and there collected Robert's parents for a visit to the hospital. They found their son looking pale but really quite cheerful. He said that with the sedative wearing off he had begun to feel some pain. It would be, he was told, several more days before the stitches came out. Then he could begin to exercise, and get his leg fully functional again. Richards excused himself after about ten minutes, saying he had business in Falmouth, and returned to collect them about half an hour later. He said he was busy the following evening, but would bring them to the hospital again on Thursday. The Pascoes, very much relieved by now, thanked him warmly.

On Saturday next, after Sandy and Joe had finished their work at the Richards', Sandy wasn't able to get back to see Margery and Tom until he had caught up with outstanding tasks at their own farm. When he did get back, Sandy could see two of the farm hands collecting faggots made from ash twigs, who positioned them to form the base for one of the hayricks. Sandy asked why they were doing this. It was to prevent mice and rats from nesting, he was told. Once the base of the rick was complete, the hands formed its bottom layer using hay. Gradually they built up each side, angled as a backward slope, which was done to shed the rainwater.

He called in on Tom, who brought him into the kitchen, where Mrs Richards gave him a drink and asked him how he and his brother had enjoyed the haymaking. He said he'd enjoyed it very much, but could see that care had to be taken when working with scythes. After chatting briefly about the accident he said he'd got to make some milk deliveries, and having finished his drink was soon on his way. When he'd made his deliveries he came back via the higher farm road in order to see how much progress the farm hands had made with the hayrick. He could see it was nearly finished. He noticed one of the hands preparing lengths of woven reed, and on asking about that was told it was for thatching the rick, which would give it further protection from the weather.

All in all, he'd learned quite a lot about haymaking and hayricks.

Sandy joins the swimming club

AFTER THE haymaking the two farms returned to their usual routines, which for Joe and Sandy meant getting back to hoeing the vegetable gardens.

For the four friends it was a busy time at school preparing for end-of-term exams, yet despite this they still managed more visits to the creek for picnics and swimming. Swimming, over the last twelve months, was something Sandy had become much stronger at. His form master had noticed this, having seen him swim under school supervision. He showed great power, but tended to tire over relatively short distances. One afternoon he took Sandy aside and asked him if he was interested in joining a club. He said he could introduce him to the instructor at the Gyllyngvase Beach Swimming Club, who might be able to help him improve his stroke technique. Sandy thought it a great idea, and agreed to meet him the following evening at Gyllyngvase beach.

There Sandy was led by his form master to a hut where a group of men and boys were changing into full-length costumes. He was introduced to George Rowe, the swimming instructor, who asked him his age and where he had learned to swim. He explained a little bit about the club. It was new, having been formed in 1887, and had seen its largest increase in membership during the last year. He placed Sandy with a group of swimmers, whom he introduced. One of these was a man called F C Lane, who was team captain and honorary secretary. Another was A C Tweedy, the club's honorary treasurer.

Sandy got himself changed (a full-length costume complete with shoulder straps), and on coming out of the hut was led by Rowe down to the water, where he was asked to do a bit of breaststroke. This he did with some power but plenty of splashing. When he got out Rowe explained where he was going wrong, and showed him some exercises that would help correct his strokes. In the next few weeks Sandy, under Rowe's instruction, improved enormously, finding himself able to swim longer distances with less effort and fatigue. After about a month Rowe went on to show him how to swim sidestroke. This Sandy managed quite well after several tries and some correction. He learned also how to life-save (the whole point of sidestroke), supporting another body supposedly in distress. By the end of July Sandy was a strong swimmer.

When he met up with his friends at the old barn towards the end of July, he asked if they wanted to join the swimming club. They all declined.

The hayrick fire

THE SUMMER was drawing to a close, and the workload at the two farms began to increase, first with the vegetable crops, then with the corn that had to be harvested. It put a stop to the four friends meeting so often. Just before harvest time, John was returning home one evening after a meeting in Falmouth. While driving along, he looked up the hill towards the Richards' farm, where first he saw a flicker of light, then flames from one of the hayricks. He heard shouting, then four youths ran across the field above the road. As he wasn't far from home, he drove hard and was soon in the yard, where he tethered the horse and rushed inside the house. His family were all sitting in the parlour quietly reading.

'The Richards!' he said. 'There's a hay rick on fire!'

Sandy and Joe grabbed what buckets they could and followed him up to the Richards' place. When the three of them reached the ricks the Richards family were already there throwing water over the blaze. Richards galvanised them quickly, getting Toye and his sons to draw water from the horse troughs and douse the two other ricks nearby, to counter the flying sparks. After what seemed an age the fire was put out, but the rick was all but destroyed. The other two, however, had been saved, due to the Toyes' prompt action. John looked around at the various members of the Richards family, and couldn't help laughing at their blackened faces, what with all the smoke and soot. Richards and his wife invited their Samaritans inside, where they shared a drink and talked about possible causes of the fire. John told them that he'd seen the flames from the lower road, and at the same time four youths running away, one of them slightly taller than the other three. From the description, Tom said he thought they were the same four who had bullied Billy Venning in Constantine.

Richards said he'd report the incident to the local police in Falmouth, and for now that's how they left it. When John and his sons arrived home his wife had already stabled the horse and was waiting for them anxiously.

About a week later Richards was informed by the police that other witnesses had also seen the four youths, who indeed proved to be the bullies of Billy Venning. They were later charged with arson.

Harvest time

THE EARLY part of August was a busy time for both farms, with harvesting underway. With Toye's farm hands fully occupied with cereal crops, Richards had to find additional labour elsewhere. A farm nearby owned by a man named Minhinick, having this year concentrated on vegetable crops, had farm hands available, six of whom were hired, after negotiation.

As it was Sandy's school holidays, he was able to keep up his swimming as well as help out with the harvest. As the weather in the first week was sunny and warm, the farm hands made good progress, cutting down the barley and oats. Sandy and Joe were tasked to bind and stook the sheaves as they were cut, which was back-breaking work. However, fit lads that they were, they soon got used to the pace.

In the second week the weather turned, with several nights of rain. This made the stooking much harder, with the wet barley spikes piercing their skin and covering their arms in sores. At last however the oats and barley were fully harvested, leaving the farm hands to rake the fields for any crop residue. Toye told his hands to go easy with this, as he wanted the local women to be allowed in, which was normal practice. This was because there was usually enough corn in the fields to make a good quantity of bread. At about this time, two of Toye's hands started building the corn-ricks, and whenever he had the chance Sandy would watch this work being done.

By mid-August Sandy's father tested the wheat in the lower field, and was delighted to find it ripe and ready for harvesting. Earlier, he'd come to the conclusion that it wouldn't be ready till the end of the month or even early September, but now, clearly, the warm sunny weather had helped it on. To harvest the wheat, his farm hands had to get used to the sickles he'd purchased earlier in the year. After a bit of practice they got the measure of it, and were soon making good progress. Again Sandy and Joe were tasked with binding and stooking, and as the stalks of wheat were much firmer this proved a great deal easier.

As before, a rick was built up with faggots, followed by sheaves of wheat. Finally the rick was thatched with reed. The corn-ricks would stay in place until the miller was ready to take the oats, barley and wheat, which he would grind into flour after threshing out the husks and chaff. John examined his ricks when they were all complete, and was satisfied with the yields. He was especially pleased with his trial wheat crop.

After the harvest some of his hands walked round one of the fields with a corn dolly they had made from a wheat sheaf. It was an old custom – a ritual of thanks for a good harvest, and the hope of more to come. John Toye smiled as he watched them.

Sandy's visit to Gunnislake

WITH THE harvest done, there was little for Sandy to do around the farm other than odd jobs. Frankly he was bored. His main problem was that Margery and Tom had been staying with relatives at Redruth for the last two weeks of the holiday, while Jim had gone with his father on a fishing trip – also for several weeks. They had taken a boat out from Helford Passage and met up with two other vessels, and were now jointly fishing for pilchards off the coast.

His rescue came in the form of a letter, which his father brought out to the yard for him to see. It was from his wife's brother, Peter Richards (no relation to their neighbours), and was an invitation to Sandy to spend a couple of weeks at their home at Gunnislake, a place on the Cornwall and Devon border. Sandy was overjoyed, especially as the Richards' son George was about his own age. They had been here on a family visit last year, and he had enjoyed George's company.

Sandy packed his clothes that evening and went to bed early, though was unable to sleep, excited as he was. In the morning after breakfast he gathered his belongings while his father brought round the horse and trap. After saying his farewells, he climbed up and off they drove to Falmouth. When they got to the railway station, Sandy's father bought him a return ticket for Tavistock and made sure he had a seat in a carriage before driving off. Now, because Sandy had never been on a train before, he was really excited when its whistle blew and smoke came belching out of its funnel, prior to it getting underway. The train passed through Penryn and then across the Carnon river by Deveron, where Sandy could see the factories and mines he knew about from that previous trip with his friends.

Next stop was Truro, Cornwall's capital, where Sandy could see large stone buildings at the centre of the town. The train pulled away only after taking on a heavy load of passengers, then resumed its journey to St Austell. At St Austell he could clearly see the china clay works in full production, with a white powder blanketing many of the surrounding features. On leaving St Austell the train made its way up the Fowey valley, where Sandy was surprised to see so many different types of crops being grown, many of which were ready to be harvested. On the whole though this part of the county contrasted with his own, being hilly and mainly used for grazing sheep and cattle.

After short stops at Lostwithiel and Liskeard the train headed for Devon and crossed the Saltash bridge, a structure designed by Brunel. Finally the train completed its journey at Plymouth, a city the size of which Sandy was amazed at. He climbed down onto the platform and was further amazed by the size of the station itself, what with so many people milling about, all destined for distant places. He managed to find his platform for the Tavistock train, and had only to wait about half an hour before it arrived. He even managed to get a seat by a window. Off they chugged in a cloud of smoke, whereupon Sandy settled back to views of the Devon countryside.

From Plymouth the train headed for Yelverton, a town on the edge of Dartmoor. The land here was mainly for grazing, but away to the east Sandy could see areas of scrub and outcrops of rocks, and, astonishingly, a very great number of ponies roaming freely on the moor.

The train finally pulled in at Tavistock, where he was met by Peter Richards with his son George, who after an exchange of greetings drove him in their trap to Gunnislake. On arriving home George showed Sandy his room, then they all sat down for their evening meal. Sandy talked about his parents, and how the harvesting had gone, and how he'd learned about building hay and corn-ricks. Then, as it was getting late, and Sandy was very tired, he excused himself and went to bed.

For a whole week George and Sandy were inseparable, exploring everywhere round Gunnislake. Then Mrs Richards took them to see Buckland Abbey, where the monks had a variety of occupations, ranging from winemaking to stonemasonry. For a treat on market day Mr Richards drove them to Tavistock, where the market burgeoned with life and trade. Outside the market was a fair, where the two boys tried their hand at most of the stalls' games, enjoying the coconut shy and hoopla most. When their money ran out they returned to the market, where Mr Richards was concluding his purchases. After a pause for lunch, which Mrs Richards had made up, they drove back to Gunnislake.

For the rest of the holiday George and Sandy played in the treehouse built by Richards on a plot of land he used mainly for grazing horses, of which he owned several, being captain of a local tin mine and therefore relatively prosperous. The holiday went all too quickly, and soon it was Sunday, the eve of Sandy's return to Falmouth. In the evening he packed his clothes. On the Monday he said his farewells, though not before inviting George to the farm. Richards brought round the horse and trap, and climbing up Sandy waved goodbye. When they got to the station they had to wait some fifteen minutes for the Plymouth train, and when it arrived Richards made sure that Sandy was settled by a window seat. The journey back to Plymouth was less interesting, Sandy having seen most of the sights on the way to Tavistock. At Plymouth he changed trains for Falmouth, and pulling out of the station he took an interest in the various house styles: some were of sandstone, some brick, and some were of limestone. On reaching the Saltash bridge into Cornwall Sandy was tired and falling asleep.

He woke just before reaching Falmouth. After a wash in the small basin in the toilet compartment he tidied himself up in readiness for his father, whom he looked out for as the train slowly drew up to the platform. Sure enough, there he was waiting. His father took his case and together they walked to the horse and trap, Sandy talking all the time about all the things he'd done on his holiday. Once back at the farm Sandy jumped down and rushed inside the house, where he regaled the whole family with the time he'd spent at Gunnislake.

Sandy is ill with measles

NEXT MORNING Sandy was allowed to get up late, so on coming down only his mother was in the kitchen. After breakfast, he told her he wasn't feeling so well – he'd got a headache and his throat was sore. She said he must have caught a cold and packed him off to bed with a hot drink.

Later that evening his father went up to see him, and noticed that his nose and throat were quite choked and his eyelids red and swollen. To him it was something more serious than a cold. He sent for the local doctor – or rather he sent his eldest son Joe in the trap to Dr Pengelly's, who lived in Constantine. When the doctor arrived, about an hour later, his examination revealed bluish-white spots ringed with red inside Sandy's mouth. These were called koplik spots, and it meant that Sandy had measles, and so had to be isolated from other children and kept in semi-darkness. Strong sunlight could impair his sight. He told Mrs Toye to administer hot vapour inhalations, as this would combat the onset of pneumonia. He'd call again tomorrow.

His examination the following day saw more obvious signs of measles, a rash now appearing on Sandy's body. He reaffirmed the need for isolation and vapour inhalations. His next visit was two days after that, when Sandy was showing signs of recovery. However, isolation in semi-darkness was still deemed necessary, and that would be the case for a further week.

With Margery, Tom and Jim having returned from *their* time away, they soon heard that Sandy was ill, and were of course anxious to see him, though were obliged to wait. By the end of the week he was allowed to get up for a few hours each evening, but it was another week after that before he was allowed out of the house. Towards the end of this quarantine period he would rise late in the morning and sit in the kitchen watching his mother preparing food. Sometimes he was allowed to help with the vegetables. One morning she was sieving warm milk, a process that removed straw and other impurities from it. She poured it into large shallow settling dishes, then left it to cool all day while she went about her other chores. The next day she skimmed off the cream that had risen on the milk, and stirred it to prevent a skin forming. She put the cream into the churn barrel and slowly turned the handle – a job that Sandy was also allowed to do, at a speed set by her. She was making butter, and explained that turning too fast would make it too soft. It was a job that took several hours, so they took it in turns.

She knew from experience how slowly to turn the barrel and when the butter was formed. Before she took it out she washed her hands first in warm water and oatmeal, then in cold water, a cleansing process that reduced any risk of tainting her produce. Then she washed the butter, to remove any last trace of buttermilk. After that she made up several packs, wrapped in muslin, which she stored in the cool cupboard. When all that was done, she turned her attention to beef and onions for the making of Cornish pasties, and pilchards for star gazy pie.

By the end of the week Sandy was up and about the farm, and although feeling much fitter was still looking pale. The doctor visited again on Friday, whereupon he pronounced that Sandy could return to school on Monday. Unfortunately for him, having missed a few weeks, he'd got a lot of catching up to do, and so for his first week back he saw Tom and Jim only briefly each day, though he did arrange to see them on the Saturday. That was the first opportunity he had to recount his adventures at Gunnislake, and to tell them what measles was like.

Not long after this his father received a letter from Peter Richards, to say that George had recently recovered from measles – he hoped that Sandy hadn't caught that illness too. You can guess the reply.

Sandy returns to the swimming club

ALTHOUGH NOT back to full fitness, Sandy resumed with the swimming club, where he was given simple exercises and short swims to build his strength gradually. After a week of this he was almost back to normal, and by the end of the season was a better swimmer than ever before, with a much improved stroke technique. On the last class of the year George Rowe asked him if he'd be coming again, to which Sandy said yes – next year he'd attend as many evenings as he could. The only times when it may not be possible were during haymaking and the corn harvest, though even then he might be able to come one night a week. So committed, Rowe gave him a list of exercises he could carry out at home during the close season.

The new gas lighting system at the manor house

THE FOLLOWING week Sandy had to help, as did Margery and Tom, with lifting the vegetable crops. It gave him a sore back but he soon got used to the bending and lifting. In the second week the workload eased off, so Sandy was able to visit his friends at home on several evenings. On one in particular, Jim had arrived before him, and Mr Richards asked the four of them if they would like to see the new gas-lighting system that had been installed at the manor house. He had been given the invitation when delivering vegetables. They were all curious to see what this new contraption was like, as their own homes were illuminated by oil lamps and candles. Tom even asked what made this new system better. His father explained that in this particular case the improvement came with the introduction of incandescent gas mantles. These were made of fabric impregnated with oxides of cerium and thorium, so that once the gas flame was burning it raised the mantles to a high enough temperature that they gave out a brilliant white light. He'd read about in a newspaper recently.

The manor house wasn't that far away, so it didn't take long to get there. Bonallack saw them coming, a tall, well built man, with black hair tinged with grey, and fierce-looking features that dissolved in a smile so soon as he greeted them. He showed them into the hall then into the drawing-room, where he turned on his gas mantles. Initially they popped, which to the visitors was a bit of a fright. They were amazed, however, at the intensity with which they glowed, and at the light that filled the room. Oil lamps just didn't compare. Yet that was more or less it, and with the demonstration over, Bonallack quizzed the four friends as to how they were getting on at school, then showed them to the kitchen where cook gave them lemonade. Richards thanked him warmly, and with all glasses drained Bonallack showed them out and wished them good evening. They all wondered if gas lighting would ever be fitted in their homes.

Halloween party

WITH BAD weather setting in at the end of October the four friends didn't meet up again until the Halloween party. This year Margery, Tom and Jim were invited to Sandy's. Margery came as a gypsy, while Tom and Jim were pirates. Sandy and Joe took on the guise of smugglers, with clothes and contraband stuffed in their pockets. Little Freddie, being a year older, this time took a more active part in the games.

Sandy's mother laid out sweetmeats, cakes and biscuits, in a room that had been cleared of most of its furniture and all of its breakables. As of the previous year, they ducked for apples and bit at treacle buns on strings while blindfolded. But there were two more games also. The first involved bird shapes cut from pieces of paper. These were placed on the floor while the players were each given rolls of paper. They had to use these rolls to beat the floor so that the draught set the birds in flight. The winner was the one who flapped his or her bird to the opposite wall of the room. They all started enthusiastically but couldn't get the birds moving straight along the floor. The players began bumping into each other, some deliberately, so that most ended up in a pile of bodies, with the birds strewn everywhere. Tom, however, who was much shrewder than the rest, was more patient, and slowly flapped his bird across to the other wall, and so won the prize.

The other new game was pass the parcel, where all the players sat in a ring on the floor. A large parcel tied with string was passed from person to person until told to stop by Sandy's father. *He* had his back to the players, and so couldn't see who had the parcel at any one time. It was slow at first, but when everyone realised how many wrappings there were they went much faster. In fact they went at a furious pace, slowing down only when the parcel had become quite small. The prize was finally won by Freddie, partly helped by Margery, who suddenly gave it to him on peeling it to its last wrapper. Under that last wrapper was a set of paints and brushes.

Firework display and musical evening

IN NOVEMBER not much went on at the two farms. All of the main crops had been lifted and stored. The days were short and dark, and the weather was blustery. However, there were two occasions of note during that month. The first one was on the 5th of November, when Sandy's class had a history lesson in the afternoon. Topically, the teacher had prepared a little talk on Guy Fawkes and the gunpowder plot of 1604. It was all still very much buzzing around in Sandy's head when school was over for the day and he began walking home. Surprisingly, his father was waiting in the wagon, not far from the school gates. Sandy ran over and patted the horse and climbed up next to his father, who told him he'd been delivering vegetables, first to the manor house, then to a trader in Falmouth. As they began the drive back home, he told him that Bonallack had invited them and the Richards family to a firework display that evening at the manor house.

After supper, and after whatever tasks they all had to do, the Toye family got themselves ready for the outing, all wrapping up warm. When they got to the manor house there was a large bonfire blazing away, with people all round it throwing on twigs and branches. Sandy immediately spotted his friends and called out to Margery and Tom. Soon everyone was together, and presently Toye and Bonallack were being introduced to each other's wives. They all had hot drinks, then huddled together as they waited for the display to start. One of Bonallack's gardeners appeared with boxes of fireworks, which were unpacked and arranged in the sequence they were going to be set off in. First came the Roman candles, a riot of colourful flame. Then came the squibs and the Catherine wheels, followed by rockets that whooshed up spectacularly into the night sky before bursting into a shower of sparks. Finally some fireworks secured to a board were set off, grouped in such a way that their flames inscribed the air with the name BONALLACK. Everyone clapped and said ah!

The other notable occasion was about a week later. Richards came over to the Toye farmhouse and invited John and his family over for supper the next Saturday, when there would be music.

For his wife's birthday he had bought a piano, knowing how well she used to play before they were married. She had so much missed playing since, only ever having the opportunity when she visited her parents. But now with her new piano, and with a bit of practice behind her, she was ready to give a rendition.

The Toyes dressed up for the occasion, and when they got there were welcomed fulsomely by Richards. While they were all taking off their hats and coats they could hear Mrs Richards playing in the parlour. When they went in, she, Margery and Tom got up to greet them. After a bit of gossip they all settled down to hear her play – mostly well-known songs. She even persuaded the menfolk to join in, who did their bit with some popular Cornish and Devonshire songs. Soon they'd all worked up an appetite, and Mrs Richards and her daughter laid on some food and hot drinks – especially delicious as Mrs Richards was such a good cook. After that she suggested that the young ones play musical chairs, for which she supplied the music. They went about it with enthusiasm, all fast and furious, and it came down finally to two players, Joe and Margery, Margery winning after Joe fell in a heap after missing the last chair. The adults roared with laughter.

When it was time to go, Mrs Richards was complimented on her playing, and after wrapping up in their heavy coats John Toye and his family made their way home, well-fed and contented.

Preparation for winter and pre-Christmas feast

BY THE beginning of December Sandy's mother had almost completed her food preparations for the winter, and had done it much more thoroughly this year in the light of her experience from the last. Now she was more confident and much more adventurous, with a greater range of preserves. She even had hams hanging in the chimney above the fire, to cure. Sometimes Sandy would help her, preparing fruit for cooking and storing in jars (when often Freddie sneaked in to the kitchen and slunk off with some of the goodies, for which he eventually got a rap on the knuckles, with a big wooden spoon).

For Sandy's father it had been a good year. He had brought the farm buildings back to a good state of repair, and his various crops, especially the wheat, had been better than expected. Moreover, he had got a good rate for his produce. His son Joe had left school and was working on the farm full-time, and showed great aptitude for the work. Satisfyingly too there was sufficient capital in the bank from the sale of his joinery business to allow for any bad years ahead. For the following year he contemplated renting additional fields, which would help him plan a better rotation of crops and allow some of his own fields to be left fallow. In respect of this, he had made an appointment for the following week with Mr Minhinick, who owned several farms in the locality. Together they reached agreement over the rental of five fields for some years ahead, so giving him much better control over long-term planning.

After drawing up his rotation plan, he went to see his senior farm hand, Jim Pollard. Jim didn't quite agree with him as to which fields should be left fallow. In his view, those that had yielded poor crops due to excessive cultivation were the ones he should choose. Toye was as ever more than happy to take his advice. Furthermore he asked him if next spring he could give him and his son Joe some instruction in ploughing, especially when it came to dealing with sloping fields, such as at the higher reaches of the farm. Jim said he'd be pleased to help. And he was encouraged, he said, that Joe was taking such an interest in farm work.

During Christmas week Elizabeth made preparations for a pre-Christmas feast, for the benefit of all her husband's hands and their families. She had hired two young girls from the village to help. On the last working day before Christmas, while Sandy was taking presents up to the Richards family, his mother and the two hired girls were setting out long tables they had borrowed from the church. This was in one of the empty barns, where they'd covered the tables with tablecloths. About an hour before the guests arrived they brought out the food and drink. On the nearest tables they put cooked chicken, hams, star gazy pies (with pilchards' heads poking out of the crusts), brawn, cooked vegetables, pickled eggs and onions, as well as bread and packs of butter. The next ones were laid with apple pies, clotted-cream buns, jellies, cakes and nuts. The others were laid with pitchers of cider, beer and lemonade.

When the guests arrived they were amazed at such a spread. Elizabeth could hear them say that John Toye's uncle never laid on a feast at all for his hands and their families, let alone one of such magnitude. It reminded them of John Toye's grandfather, who was generous unlike Benjamin, though the latter did give them a Christmas bonus. Everyone really enjoyed the meal, and after it Toye gave his hands their annual bonuses, Jim getting extra for all the help and advice he had given. Some people even got a little tipsy.

On Christmas day Sandy's mother cooked an excellent repast, and the rest of the day they spent quietly, after opening their presents. For what was left of December and for the whole of January the weather was bitterly cold and the roads icy. Only a minimum of maintenance work was carried out around the farm.

On returning to school, Sandy and Freddie were taken and collected by their father, as the roads were so treacherous and the weather so biting. Everyone yearned for spring.

Visit to the blacksmith's shop and sledging in the snow

ONE SATURDAY morning at the end of January Sandy woke up early and looked out of the window. To his astonishment several inches of snow had fallen in the night. Where it powdered the trees it had frozen, and now in the full light of morning sparkled in the sunshine. He dressed quickly, as he wanted his breakfast early, keen to go out and play in the snow. Joe and Fred had already eaten their breakfast and were outside throwing snowballs. Sandy was soon out with them, where Joe had a distinct advantage, being older and stronger and able to throw the snowballs longer distances. However, all of them soon had to come indoors, as they were getting wet and chilled to the bone. They changed and were given hot drinks.

Later that morning Sandy was asked by his father to take their horse to the blacksmith near Falmouth, because of a broken shoe that needed to be replaced. He would also have to check the hoof for injury. He was careful as he drove to Falmouth, but managed to get there without any mishap. At the smithy's the coals were a red-hot glow, with the smithy himself bent over the fire, holding a long iron bar. A young lad operated the bellows. This was the blacksmith's apprentice, a tall scrawny boy with spiky fair hair. His face was pimply with adolescence, and was very red through the job that he did. To Sandy, he didn't look strong enough for this kind of work. The smith himself was too preoccupied with what he was doing to see Sandy. He was dark haired, swarthy and of medium height, and strongly built, with large muscular arms. The fire made him sweat profusely, which glistened on his face and arms. Even his vest was soaked. He pulled out the rod from the fire with a gloved hand, and beat it on the anvil with a hammer. When he'd got the shape he wanted he quenched it in a tank of water. Sandy looked around. To him it was like an Aladdin's cave, with so many interesting things hanging on the walls or lying on the shelves. There were horses' harnesses, and brasses, and copper pots that reflected the glow of the fire. There were locks and keys, also caught by the light from the fire. On the floor were boxes of nails, ornaments brought here for repair, and a good many of the blacksmith's tools.

At last the blacksmith caught sight of him. He knew Sandy from work he had done at the farm, and after polite enquiries as to his family asked him what he wanted. Sandy showed him the broken shoe. With not much effort the blacksmith had the shoe off and examined the horse's hoof and leg. There was no injury, he said, and he cleaned the hoof with a file. After checking the size of the shoe he fetched one similar and nailed it on. There was nothing to pay now, the blacksmith told him – he would see his father later.

Just before leaving, Sandy saw in a corner, behind a kibble under repair, two long sledges, built with iron frames and wooden boards. He asked if he could borrow them. The blacksmith replied that Sandy could have them to keep: his sons, who had used them years ago, were now grown men and in any case no longer lived nearby. So, with the sledges in the cart, Sandy drove back home, where he showed off his prizes. In the afternoon he and Joe tried them out on the hill above the farm, and found them fast, light and well balanced. They had great fun, sledging in the deepest snow till well after dusk. On the Sunday morning, Sandy was due to meet his three friends at the Richards' farm, and so took the sledges with him. In no time at all they were all hauling them to the top of the hill, Jim and Margery coming down on one, Sandy and Tom on the other. Sometimes one pair would try to go too fast, and the sledge would veer off the track and end up buried in the snow, under a tumble of arms and legs, much to the others' laughter. After an hour of this the friends decided they would have one last turn, and Jim and Margery challenged the other two to a race. They'd start from the highest part of the hill and career on down past the farmhouse.

They dragged their sledges up to the top of the hill and set off together. For several yards it was neck and neck, with neither sledge able to get a lead. Gradually Jim and Margery drew ahead, their combined weight being less than that of the other two. Quite apart from that, Jim was much better at steering. In one final effort to catch up, Tom directed his sledge over the high side of the hill, at which point he started to gain ground with the steepness of the slope. Suddenly the sledge hit a protruding stone and started to wobble, and despite all Tom's best efforts veered off the track and hit a tree. Tom, who was at the front, was flung forward onto the tree and hit it with his shoulder. Sandy, luckily for him, was tossed into the deep snow and escaped unhurt. Margery and Jim, now at the bottom of the hill, had seen everything. They ran up the track to see how badly Tom was hurt. Fortunately he wasn't much hurt at all, and all that befell Sandy was a good soaking.

They helped Tom down the hill to the Richards' farmhouse, where his mother examined the shoulder and found it only slightly bruised. She washed his face, which some low branches of the tree had scratched. Then he was put to bed. The other three said that they'd enjoyed the day's sledging and were thankful that the accident hadn't been worse.

Lost Sheep at the Richards' Farm

THAT EVENING at the Toyes' place, just as everyone was settling down to read, there was a knock at the front door. John

Toye got up and was surprised to see Sid Richards. He was perturbed and out of breath. He wanted help recovering a number of his sheep lost in the snow, and it was vital to find them and dig them out before they died. 'We're with you,' said John. He said he would send for his hands in the village, and in the meantime he and his two older sons would join the search. He called out for Sandy and Joe, and told them to pick up some shovels and go on ahead of him to the Richards' farm. Then he hastened over to Jim Pollard's cottage nearby. Luckily Jim was at home, and was able to round up the other hands quickly. By the time they all got over to the Richards' place, some of the sheep had been found and put in their pens. Richards asked Jim to take half the men and search on higher ground, while John and his group went by a separate way, where they soon found more sheep sheltered by a large tree, but half buried in snow nevertheless. Quickly they dragged them out and took them back to their pens. Daylight was now beginning to fade, and they trudged through the snow to an escarpment, where someone had reported movement. Here there were more sheep – quite a lot of them – sheltering in the hollow of a rock. They cleared away a huge mound and gradually dragged the first of the sheep out, moving them to a safer spot, where they could be picked up later. They continued to dig, and unfortunately two more they found were dead.

Jim had now gone, but back at the farmhouse the rest of them had hot drinks. Richards felt especially grateful to Jim, who had so expertly organised his part of the search. He told John he'd been caught by the very heavy snows on Friday and Saturday, but had there been more warning he would have moved his flocks into their pens beforehand. They finished off their drinks, then John and his sons began walking down the hill for home. They caught up with Jim on the way, so John was able to tell him how grateful Richards was for his help.

When they were safely home, Elizabeth had got them a hot snack.

They changed out of their wet clothes and went into the kitchen, where they all tucked in heartily. It had been a long night, trudging through the snow and shovelling out to free the sheep. Afterwards they retired to the parlour, where Freddie was playing with the blocks he'd had for Christmas. Then it was early to bed for everyone.

Sandy finds Celtic remains

HEAVY SNOW fell for several days at the beginning of the following week, and when it eased Sandy and Joe were sent out to shovel it away around the area of the farmhouse. Nearer the end of the week a rapid thaw set in and water began to pour down the hill roads.

On the Friday evening, while the Toyes were eating their meal, there was a heavy rumbling and the crash of trees close to the farmhouse. John, Sandy and Joe rushed out, and saw immediately that a part of the hill on the east side had caved in under the weight of wet snow, and that the trees on the downward path had been swept away. They put on their coats and went over to inspect the damage. They found that the top end of the road was completely blocked by rocks and debris and mounds of snow. 'Not much we can do this evening,' their father said. He told them that straight after breakfast tomorrow he would round up the farm hands and use the wagons to move the debris away, and dump it in the hedgerows. When he met Jim early the next morning, Jim it was who rounded up the hands and organised the work. The rocks and stones that they loaded onto the wagons they took to the farmyard, where they could store them for later use, repairing the hedgerows around the farm. Sandy and Joe helped with this task, moving some of them into place now, where the rock-fall had damaged the hedges. When there was a lull in the work Sandy and Joe took a rest and ate from the snack that their mother had prepared for them the previous evening.

Out of curiosity, Sandy climbed over the remaining piles of rocks and looked in the hollow they'd left behind. At the bottom he could see part of a granite column protruding from the rubbish, adorned with a marking. He climbed down and found some fragments of earthenware pottery scattered about. He lifted the end of the column, and as he did so two slabs slid away, revealing a shallow chamber complete with a human skeleton. Spooked by this, he called his father over, who saw instantly what had happened. 'Don't worry,' he said. 'Whoever that is, he's been dead for hundreds of years.' He moved the slabs and saw that the skeleton reclined in a cist. Sandy, when he'd recovered from his shock, helped his father completely unearth the column, whose markings they looked at closely. Sandy said he'd seen something similar on standing stones in other parts of Cornwall. John said he thought they were Celtic in origin, and because he knew an archaeologist in Truro he would ask him to come and examine the site. He covered the whole thing up with branches – safe from prying eyes, he said – and by the time they had climbed back up to the road the two wagons had returned for another load of stones. It took something like an hour or more to clear up what remained of the rock-fall, but when the hands went back to the farmyard, John and Sandy hung back, filling in Joe on what they had found. It was important, the three of them felt, not to let the hands know anything at all about it, as the news would soon be all round the village.

An archaeologist examines the Celtic burial site

WHEN HE returned to school on Monday Sandy confided in his classmates, describing what he'd found in the hollow in all its gory detail. He didn't reveal the exact location, though he did add that his father was inviting in an archaeologist from Truro. At the midday break he saw Tom and Jim and told them about it too, whose first reaction was an eagerness to see the stone and the skeleton. Sandy said they may be able to see it on Saturday. When Sandy got home from school he checked with his father that this was all right, who said that it was as long as they didn't disturb any of the artefacts that had been uncovered. He wanted the archaeologist to see the site exactly as it was after the rock-fall. He added that he was going along there this evening himself, to ensure that no one had visited the site, and Sandy was allowed to come along too – as long as he could make himself ready in half an hour's time. He changed quickly from his school clothes, and before they set off had some cake and a hot drink in the kitchen.

Soon they were on their way. When they got to the hollow they could see that the site had not been disturbed, and that the stone and skeleton were still under the temporary covering they'd made with branches.

Next day John had business in Falmouth, and afterwards he drove on to see Mr Jago, the archaeologist who lived in Truro. Jago invited him in and said he was recovering from a cold: normally he'd be in his workshop or the museum at this time of the day. John gave him details of the rock-fall and what that had uncovered, and that made Mr Jago excited. He'd come over on the following Monday, he said – with his business commitments he couldn't make it any earlier, and anyway wanted to be clear of his cold. John thanked him and gave him directions to his farm. That evening he told his family what had been arranged, and emphasised that it was more than ever important now not to disturb the site.

On the Saturday Sandy met up with his friends at the Richards' place. Tom was still very keen on the visit, but Margery didn't like the sound of a burial site, and anyway had to help her mother in the kitchen. So, it was down to Tom, Jim and Sandy, who set out in a swirling mist. When they got to the site they found that the covering had been removed to one side. From where they stood, atop the pile of rocks, the skeleton appeared to float in the mist, a Gothic overtone they found really quite scary. They were naturally hesitant about climbing down, but when the mist parted slightly Sandy scrambled down into the pit of the tomb. A little less intrepid, Tom and Jim followed. The stone pillar with its markings remained a curiosity. The skeleton, when they looked at it more closely, they saw was laid in a cist that had been formed of stone slabs slotted together with grooves. It didn't seem to have been touched. On a closer look round, Sandy found two small circular stones with markings similar to those on the column. He lifted them out, and as the site had clearly been discovered by someone else, he felt he should take these back to his father for safekeeping.

The mist rolled in again, which lent the skeleton an ethereal look. They climbed out quickly and headed back to the road. How old, they wondered, might the monument be? Sandy said he thought it belonged to the Celtic age (whenever that was).

Back at the farmhouse Sandy sought out his father, who was working in the top barn, and showed him the stones, telling him why he'd removed them. John said he was right to have done so, as the last thing they wanted was to see them stolen. He'd go out there himself later and make a better job of covering the whole thing up.

On the Monday morning Mr Jago drove in in his wagon, with two helpers on board. It was about ten o'clock. Toye and Pollard met them at the entrance to the yard. Then they all went over to the burial site, where Jago made a thorough examination. Presently he called John down, and showed him some strings of polished stones to the side of the skeleton and the small marked stones at its feet. John asked him how old it all was. Jago thought for a while, then confirmed that the monument was Celtic, as was the cist, which, having been sealed with tight-fitting slabs, had kept the skeleton in a good state of preservation. Despite that however the skull and bones were soft, and they would deteriorate quickly if they remained exposed to the open air. He asked if he could take the stone, some samples of the pottery, the cist and the skeleton back to his workshop. John said he would have preferred that anyway, as left where they were it was only a matter of time before they were plundered.

They loaded it all up onto Jago's wagon, then drove back to the farmhouse, where John now produced the two circular stones that Sandy had found. Jago looked at them and said their markings were new to him. Before he left, Jago said he would write to John once he'd completed a more careful examination. That would be in about a week's time. Good as his word, John did indeed receive a letter. It confirmed again that the long and circular stones were Celtic, and that the cist and other artefacts were of the same period. It was difficult to give the age of the skeleton, but on the evidence of the cist it probably dated from 700 BC. The stone markings indicated that the site was a settlement of one of the tribes of Dumnonia. John read out the letter to his family, and said it had all been quite a discovery.

Ploughing with the arrival of spring

IN MARCH the weather was much milder, and that allowed John and his sons and the farm hands to prepare the fields for ploughing. Again, as in the previous year, there were large stones that had to be removed from the fields. The drains too needed clearing again, and some demanded repair. While this was being done, Pollard and the other hands prepared the equipment for ploughing.

When ploughing did at last commence, as promised Jim showed John and his son Joe the basics of ploughing technique, and it wasn't long before he was able to leave them alone with one of the lower, flatter fields. He, meanwhile, took on one of the more difficult sloping fields, which last year had been left fallow. John couldn't help feeling proud of his son, for Joe was now taking an active interest in all the work that had to be done, and talked at length about what crops they would grow. Sandy, by contrast – although he worked hard at whatever he was asked to do – was less interested himself in being a farmer. He'd often said that instead he wanted to go to sea, and travel the world.

By the end of the week Joe and his father had become competent ploughmen, at least on the flat – in fact their contribution was such that more than half the fields were done. On the following Monday John was given details of the forthcoming ploughing competition at Truro. He passed the information on to Jim Pollard, saying he was quite happy for him to take part. Later, when he told his family – and before his sons had a chance to plead that they too wanted to go – he told them about his plans to enter Jim, and that naturally they'd all go along and watch.

By the end of the second week the ploughing was finished and the fields were ready for planting.

On Saturday morning, the day of the competition, the family set off for Truro, with picnic hampers stowed in the wagon. When they got there they could see Jim making preparations for his turn in the competition. They joined Jim's family, and while the others unloaded the wagon John went over to his senior hand and wished him success. When they'd had their picnic, the Toyes and the Pollards strolled among the stalls and amusements, having goes at various things.

John stayed and watched the ploughing competition. Of the ten competitors, Jim and last year's winner really stood out, Jim having improved a lot since then. He was now much more experienced, and that had bolstered his confidence. He went through his paces, showing little fault. When it was his rival's turn, he started well, showing the judges just how good he was, but then at a late stage unexpectedly allowed the plough to slip – possibly through over-confidence. From there he found it difficult to recover a good line. Nevertheless, he completed with a good finish.

When the result was declared, Jim had won by half a point. John shook his hand firmly and warmly congratulated him. After the prize-giving, they joined the others and helped them demolish the remains of the picnic. Then they loaded up the wagons and drove off on their separate ways home, shouting their farewells. For John the day had been great fun and a huge success, for the fact that one of his hands had won the competition would not go unnoticed among the rest of the farming community.

The next week turned John's joy to worry as one of his South Devon cows was having difficulty calving. The cow was sweating heavily and wasn't at all comfortable. He knew South Devons did sometimes have this kind of difficulty, but he couldn't be sure exactly what the problem was. He watched on anxiously for two evenings, then called in Jim Pollard to help. Jim was able to deduce that there were problems with the position of the calf, its head not being in quite the right place. He showed him how to reach inside and make the necessary correction.

The next day John had to make that same correction again, and when Jim visited in the evening all was looking well: he expected the cow to give birth that night. They took it in turns to keep watch. In the early hours of the morning, when John returned to the barn to take another turn, he was greeted by Jim rushing out, who told him that the birth was imminent and that they would need to help the calf along its way. The cow was in difficulties, so Jim tied her fore feet with rope, which he secured to the barn. The two of them then hauled the calf out. After untying the rope, they washed the calf, and with that job done Jim told him he'd got a fine heifer to add to his stock. While the calf was feeding, John reflected just how invaluable Jim must have been to his Uncle Benjamin, for surely without him the farm would not have survived. Once again, he owed him a debt of thanks.

Sandy finds a smugglers' hoard

APRIL 1890, and the weather was cold with high winds and periods of rain. This didn't stop the four friends planning their trips to the creek and other places. On one such occasion they decided to take a tent and stay overnight at the creek. Jim collected them early on a Friday evening, so they got there well before it was dark. Sandy brought cheeses, milk and boiled eggs, while Margery and Tom had ham, pickles and bread. Jim brought some fish, which they would all have fun cooking.

They pitched the tent, which they'd borrowed from Sandy's father, in the field above the creek. This proved to be a difficult job, as the wind was anything but gentle. However, with Margery and Tom securing the guide ropes, and the others wrestling with the canvas, they finally succeeded. When they'd got everything inside, Sandy and Jim climbed down to the beach and gathered driftwood and dry grasses to make a fire. When the fire was roaring luxuriantly Jim brought out his fish and a pan and started cooking. The others meanwhile sorted out the ham, bread, cheeses and pickles, and soon all of them were gorging themselves.

When, later, it was getting dark, they all huddled in the tent while Jim set up an oil lamp, whose light flickered eerily on the walls. They made figures casting shadows with their fingers, all the while listening to the wind outside soughing in the trees. Presently they went to bed. The next morning they all rose early, Jim going down to the beach to re-light the fire with a new bundle of driftwood. He heated water in a can and made some tea, which he took back to the tent, where he filled up everyone's mug. It was warmer today, so they all sat outside drinking their tea and eating what was left of their provisions.

After breakfast Margery, Tom and Jim climbed down to the beach. There they took off their stockings and boots and paddled in the cold water lapping in the creek. Sandy preferred to explore the top of the cliff above the beach, but as he walked along he got his boot caught in a tangle of grass growing in a soft clump of sand. He fell heavily, right on the cliff face, sending heaps of sand to the beach below. Luckily he wasn't hurt, and when he picked himself up he could see a large hole where part of the cliff had collapsed. When he got closer he could see it was man-made, being lined with timbers for support. In fact it was a cave, into which he descended. Inside there were crates filled with bottles, and only partly covered by sand. He could tell by the smell that it was brandy. He went further in and found a sack secured with cord. When he opened it, it was stuffed with coins, of silver and gold.

Hardly able to contain his excitement, he heaved the sack out and took it up to the others, who by now had left the creek. They were staggered and amazed at the sheer number of coins he had found. Jim said there must be nearly a hundred. Together they shipped out the brandy and together with the sack loaded it onto the cart. Sandy spread the coins out on a sheet, and saw that some of them were over a hundred years old. It all smacked suspiciously of smugglers, whose booty had been there quite possibly for over a century. The best thing they could do, Sandy said, was hand the whole lot over to the authorities. If there was a reward, he'd share it with them. Jim advised it was best to return to Sandy's house first. They took down the tent, got everything onto the cart and set off.

Soon they were on their way back to the Toyes' farm, their heads full of images of smugglers past, all with black beards and eye patches. Sandy's mother came out from the farmhouse and asked why they had come back so early. Sandy could hardly contain himself when he told her. While they unloaded the cart, she went and found her husband in one of the barns. He came out and took a look at the coins, which he declared quite a find, and said that they certainly looked valuable. Over the weekend he would lock them and the brandy away, and would think about how to notify the authorities – perhaps on Monday morning.

A trip to St Michael's Mount

ONE DAY during the Easter holiday Sandy was asked by his father if he wanted to go to St Michael's Mount. It had to be Sandy on his own, because Freddie was still too young and Joe was busy planting vegetable seeds. Sandy said he would like to go, as he had heard so much about the Mount and its history. His father had planned a trip for the following Thursday to the market at Marizion, and as that was near St Michael's Mount they would visit then. When the day came around they had an early breakfast, then set off on the twenty-mile ride – which in the horse and trap would take about two hours.

The weather was dry, cold and very blustery, and they had to wrap up well. As it was springtime, daffodils bloomed in the hedgerows, and bluebells carpeted the woodlands. After passing through Helston the road turned south and followed the coastline. Then came the picturesque villages of Breage and Ashton. At Germoe they could look south to the Praa Sands, which stretched for about a mile along that part of the coast. Finally they were on the Marizion road, having made good time for the market. They headed for what his father called Marketjew, which made up part of Marizion (Marizion was made up of two hamlets, Marketjew and Marizion itself). In Marketjew they visited a shop selling fabrics, hats and haberdashery. The shopkeeper was Jewish, and knew Sandy's father well, as the two men greeted each other warmly. Soon they got down to business – the sale of some cloth for a suit. After quite some haggling they agreed on a price, at which point the shopkeeper cut the cloth and wrapped it in brown paper. With the business concluded, Sandy and his father said their goodbyes, and were soon back on the road, heading for St Michael's Mount. Once there, they stopped at the causeway, where the horse and trap could be stabled.

As it was low tide they were able to walk across the causeway all the way to the Mount. Underfoot they came upon a cross shape that had been cut into one of the causeway slabs. John told his son that it was believed a metal cross had once been inserted in the slab, but at some point had been lost or stolen. When they reached the lower part of the Mount they headed for the house of one of its staff, who could show them round. John had known him from his previous employment as crew member in a fishing boat that plied from Falmouth. When they called he was at home, fortunately, and pleased to see them, and more than happy to show them round the castle. He'd show them the rest of the Mount for that matter, but before all that he had some work to complete. While he was away his wife made some tea and got out some cakes. When the guide got back he led them up to the church, warning them to watch out for the chunks of granite that could so easily injure them if they slipped and fell.

Part way up he showed them an old well. This he said was linked to a famous legend about Jack the giant-killer. This was all about a local Cornishman, who thought out a way of killing the giant Cormoran, who lived on the Mount and was terrorising the neighbourhood. Jack went to the Mount early one morning and dug a huge pit, then, just as the sun was rising, he blew his horn. The giant woke and in a rage at being roused so early rushed down the Mount. As the sun was in his eyes he couldn't see much ahead of him and so fell into the pit, breaking his neck in the process, and dying shortly afterwards.

The guide said there was a grave on a high part of the Mount, which from its size belonged to a man who was extremely large and tall. The body had been removed some time after it was first buried and re-interred in the cemetery. Naturally this was thought by some to be the giant. Next they looked round the church, and followed that with the castle. The Mount, Sandy learned, had been home in various times of war to persons such as the Earl of Oxford (in the time of Richard the Lion Heart), King John when he was Regent, and also by the royalists when besieged by Cromwell's army. Here too was the rock whereon the archangel St Michael was supposedly seen by a fisherman from his boat below in the bay.

With the tour over, Sandy's father thanked the guide and gave him some silver coins for his trouble. On the way back down to the causeway John looked in at the St Aubyn Arms, but finding the inn overcrowded with folk from the market decided they would cross to Marizion and collect the horse and trap, and get ready to depart. He told Sandy he had business in Penzance, which was only three miles away. There they could get a meal at the Park Inn Hotel – a place quite near the warehouse where he had some articles to collect. Sandy was pleased with that decision, as he'd not seen Penzance before.

When they got to the hotel they made for the lounge bar,

which Sandy's father said would be so much more comfortable. It was, however, crowded, full of hubbub and noise and the smell of beer and tobacco smoke. Sandy looked about and could see that many people here were old fishermen. Quite a number weren't local, and spoke a foreign language. Some had serious injuries – one had lost an eye, another sported a deep scar right across his face, while many others had badly gnarled hands due to the work they did in the severest conditions. A tall, gaunt-looking man in a corner had an arm missing, and the person he was with did not have the full complement of fingers on one of his hands. Moreover he was restless and looking furtive.

The fishermen smoked clay pipes mostly, and that's why the room was thick with haze. Sandy could so easily see them as the old crew from one of Blackbeard's pirate ships. One of them passed quite close to him on his way to the bar, his hips very stiff as he walked. He'd got a ruddy face, was unshaven, and had a large wart on the end of his nose. Sandy was glad to sit down in a quiet corner while his father ordered their lunch. The proprietor, a large-boned jolly-looking man, with brown hair arranged to disguise his baldness, knew Sandy's father from previous visits to the hotel. He had a warm welcome for him and asked after his family and farm. John told him things couldn't be better, apart from Sandy's measles last summer. He pointed out his son, sitting in a corner. 'A fine-looking lad,' the proprietor said. John ordered hot pies, a pint of ale and a lemonade.

While waiting for the pies John politely nodded to a man propping the bar next to him, quietly drinking beer. They got into conversation, where he learned that the man was a commercial traveller selling kitchen utensils. He was of medium height with a large head and very rosy cheeks. He wore a loud check suit and his large round belly protruded over his waistband. He was loud when he talked and he laughed a lot. When John was at last served with his pies he was able to extricate himself, and took these and the drinks on a tray over to where Sandy was sitting. As they were famished, the pies didn't last long.

Sandy took a closer look around the room. There was an enormously long bar with racks for both food and glasses and tankards. At the centre of the room was a large heavy mahogany table, highly polished but despoiled by burns from whole generations of clay pipes, carelessly laid down, not to mention the rings imparted by wet glasses. The doors were of heavy dark oak, glazed at the top. The ceiling was a maze of darkly stained beams. On the walls were holders for gas lamps, but the poor lighting generally could be claustrophobic one moment and warm and cosy the next.

Before going home, they dropped in at the warehouse for John's purchases, then set off back to the farm in the late afternoon. It was after sunset when they arrived, and Sandy couldn't get inside fast enough, to tell everyone all about his adventure: St Michael's Mount, Jack the giant-killer, all those bizarre-looking fishermen at the Park Inn Hotel. They had to calm him down, while his father watched on patiently and smiled.

The Helston flora dance

IT WAS inclement weather again at the end of April, but when the four friends met at the old barn (as usual) their main topic of conversation was the forthcoming flora day, a celebration taking place on the 8th of May at Helston. They planned to head over there at about nine o'clock, as it would take them over an hour. They would have left earlier, had the hal-an-tow still been part of the programme. A servants' dance, this had been dropped several years earlier, when too many of the participants were rowdy and drunk, much to the disgust of the locals. Margery would prepare the picnic, even though there would be victuals on sale. That meant they could save their money for delicacies such as shellfish or clotted cream buns. The main dance was called the furry or foddy, and that took place at midday. It was important to find a good place to stand and watch.

Helston was about ten miles away. The journey passed quickly enough, however, as the four friends had plenty to chat about practically all the way. When they were just coming in to Helston, Jim said that most of the stalls would be in Coinagehall Street and others adjacent to it. Margery had made some lily-of-the-valley sprays the previous evening, and pinned one on herself and the others on to the three lads just as they rumbled into town.

The streets were a mass of colour, adorned with cut flowers in all the houses and shop-fronts. Even against warehouse walls up many a shadowy passage there were rhododendron cuttings. They made their way to Coinagehall Street and meandered among the stalls. The lads bought toffee apples and Margery a clotted cream bun. Then at the gypsy's tent Margery decided to have her fortune told, and was in there for five or ten minutes. She came out smiling, but wouldn't tell the lads what was in store for her. After that they went to the fairground, and there had a go on the helter-skelter, the swings and the hoopla stall. Then it was the coconut shy. Tom, who was the tallest and strongest, threw first, but so wildly that he missed the coconuts completely. The others too failed to knock any of the coconuts out of their cups. Tom had another go and this time took more care with his aim, and in the end did manage to win a coconut. Margery had another go at the hoopla and won a small doll. Further along the street they found a group of young children enjoying a Punch and Judy show, which they watched for a while. By now however they had an appetite, and so made their way to where they'd left the pony and trap and set about the picnic.

It was now warm and sunny and after their picnic the four friends lay about on the grass. Then they made their way back to the town centre where the local gentry were about to perform the furry dance. It was about midday. They found themselves a good position, and when the procession was about to begin there were more than a hundred people waiting. The dancers appeared – gentlemen dressed in top hat and tails, the ladies in dazzling summer dresses. They proceeded along Meneage Street, with the band ahead of them playing the music that went with the furry dance. In and out of the houses and shops these ladies and gentlemen danced, which sometimes made it too difficult for the big drum to negotiate the narrow passages. From afar the dancers seemed to move like an enormously long serpent, swaying to the music.

When they got as far as Church Street, they danced into the grounds of Lismore, the band now increasing its tempo. They wound in an ever-decreasing circle, becoming tighter and tighter, and ending in a spiral in which they couldn't move at all. When the dancers finally broke out, all looking very tired, that completed the dance. For a moment all was deathly hush, the crowd seeming to sense a change in the air, or a fresh start to the year. The four friends broke from the crowd and returned to the stalls again, where they bought shellfish, buns and sweetmeats, then strolled on to the fair once more, where they further sampled its amusements.

Haymaking. And Sandy rescues someone drowning

JUNE WAS sunny and warm, ideal for mowing the hay, and this year John and his sons Joe and Sandy were more than competent with their scythes. They and the farm hands made short work of it. Sandy asked his father if he could help with the hayricks.

'I'll ask Jim,' he said. Pollard, initially, was hesitant, as this kind of work demanded experience. Sandy said that he'd watched it being done last year and felt that he could handle it. At this Jim relented. 'If nothing else it'll give you good experience,' he said. John was quietly pleased, as up to now Sandy, although a hard worker, did chores about the place only when told to.

Sandy went with Jim to where the other hands were marking out a position for the ricks. Jim left him to their good care, and Sandy's first job was to gather faggots for building the base. When he'd done that he was shown how the base was built, not only with strength enough to support the hay, but to prevent rats and mice from nesting. It didn't take Sandy long to learn these skills. Next they showed him how to lay on the hay and build up the rick so that it didn't overbalance. During the evenings and weekend that followed Sandy was shown how to slope the rick's walls against the rain, then how to thatch the top with reeds. When the rick was complete he was pleased with his efforts and with everything he'd learned.

For his leisure he kept up his training at the Gyllyngvase Swimming Club, and found himself able to swim greater and greater distances without getting tired. He received more instruction in stroke technique and learned correct breathing. Come July, he was a very competent swimmer, so that Rowe now decided to induct him as a life-saver – pulling out someone in trouble and applying artificial respiration. This proved vital on one occasion. It was the end of a swimming session, and Rowe shouted for all swimmers to come to the shore. Sandy was quite far out, having embarked on a long swim, but on turning for the shore he saw one of the other swimmers in quite a bit of difficulty. It was a boy, a beginner, who had swum too far out for his own good, and had got himself in a panic. Instead of flipping over on his back and just floating to gather his thoughts, he threw up his arms in desperation and shouted for help, thrashing about in the water. Pretty soon he started to go under. Sandy swam powerfully towards him, and on reaching him dived under and brought him to the surface. By this time the boy was unconscious, having swallowed too much water.

He managed to turn the boy on his back and support his head while turning over on his own back. With his own body supporting the boy he kicked his legs and stroked with one arm, thus slowly easing to the shallows. The other swimmers now saw what had happened and ran to help, and soon fished them both out onto the beach. As soon as the boy was lying down Sandy turned him on his side and checked his mouth to clear any debris that might be there. Then he applied pressure to the chest repeatedly with his hands, which pushed the seawater out of his lungs. The boy was then turned onto his back and the same rhythmic pressure was applied to his chest. After what seemed an age the boy coughed and started to breathe freely again.

All this time George Rowe was watching over Sandy, to see that what he did was right. He patted him on the back when the boy recovered, with a 'Well done, Sandy, very well done.' Sandy was surprised to see him there, having been so thoroughly engrossed in saving the boy's life. His name was John Minhinick. They took him to the hut and towelled him hard to warm him up and counteract the shock. John soon recovered his composure and thanked Sandy for saving his life. Nevertheless, Rowe took him to the local hospital, to have him checked out properly, and afterwards took him home. There the boy's father expressed his astonishment and rage that the swimmers were evidently not that well supervised, and bade George Rowe a harsh goodnight as he slammed the door in his face.

After he had changed and gone home, Sandy didn't tell either his parents or his brothers about what had happened, and after a hot drink went to bed. The next evening Sandy and his brother

Joe were in their rooms reading, Freddie was asleep in bed, and John and his wife were quietly chatting in the parlour. There was a knock at the door. John got up and was surprised to see William Minhinick, the man from whom he rented some fields. Here was an impressive figure, over six feet tall, with dark curly hair peppered with grey. He had a slight stoop from working in an office, though his face was distinguished, stern and serious – especially tonight. John assumed he'd come on business about the fields, but Minhinick told him it was to see Sandy about something very very important. Next assumption was that Sandy was in some sort of trouble, but he called him down anyway. His voice had an edge, and to Sandy that sounded ominous. When he came down into the parlour he was surprised at the presence of Mr Minhinick, a man he had seen only once before (talking to his father). Minhinick immediately rose from his chair, and crossing the room shook Sandy warmly by the hand. 'I have to thank you so much,' he said, 'for saving my son's life.'

Minhinick saw immediately that this was all news to John and his wife, so he related the story to them, from beginning to end. Sandy couldn't help feeling embarrassed. He said that anyone at the club, trained as a life-saver, would have done exactly the same. Minhinick had none of it. He was indebted to Sandy, and if there was anything at all he could do for him he only had to ask. Sandy thought about this carefully, but finally plucked up courage. 'You own several fishing boats,' he said. 'How about a fishing trip during the summer school holiday…'

'Consider it done!' Minhinick replied. 'I'll arrange it with your father next week.'

John and his wife were so pleased with the news that they thanked Mr Minhinick for coming. Once he'd been shown out, John congratulated his son and told him he was so proud of his achievement, though rebuked him warmly for not having mentioned it. Sandy only grinned awkwardly, and still a little embarrassed went back to his room. He did however really look forward to the fishing trip.

The friends find a smugglers' cave and tunnel

WITH JOHN'S new crop rotation system, only a limited number of cereals could be grown this year. Other than a few fields planted with barley and oats, most were devoted to root crops. The rest were sown with grass seed for hay production.

With a lull in the farm work and boat repairs, the four friends were able to visit the creek during the summer weekends. On one occasion, they decided again to take the tent. Almost the first thing they did was go for a swim, Sandy going far out while the others stayed in the shallows or dived off rocks. When he got back to the beach they all got dressed and climbed the cliff back to the tent, but after a while Sandy said he was going to explore some way beyond the place where they'd previously found the smugglers' hoard. The others said they'd go with him, so they all set off. They walked along the cliff-top for about half a mile, until Sandy, who was ahead of the others, saw a track leading down. When he reached its end he could see an opening in the cliff face. When the others caught up he was already pulling away the ivy that covered a hole in the cliff. When they looked closer, they could see it led to a cave. They tumbled in, and even though the light was poor they could see the cavern went well under the cliff.

As they didn't have a light or a rope they decided not to explore any further, and as it was now late in the evening they decided to go back to their camp. They would return to the cave the next day. Next morning they rose early and after a hurried breakfast went back to the cave, complete with provisions, a rope and an oil lamp. Jim shone the light in front of them. They were surprised by what they saw. Not only was this a cave, it fanned out to a tunnel with a wide roadway hewn in the solid rock. The tunnel, which sloped upwards, was lined with hooks. Sandy went ahead and wrapped the rope around one of the hooks, to make it an easier climb for the others. The floor was slippery, with a steady flow of water running from above. He slipped a couple of times but recovered and managed to make it to the top. The others followed, Sandy holding on to the rope.

He could see chinks of light above him slanting through gaps in the boards that closed the end of the tunnel directly above him. He pushed the boards aside, then, standing up straight, could see that the end of the tunnel fed in to a one-storey stone building, long made derelict. When the others caught up they found that the building was in a field a short distance from the edge of the cliff. Jim turned the light on every corner and could see that the place was stashed with old brandy kegs and sacks lying on the earthen floor. Sandy said the building must have been used by smugglers in the past, and these were the remains of their contraband. Jim, who had climbed into the building last, agreed, saying he could see scoring on the rock floor where possibly heavy loads had been dragged up the tunnel.

When the four friends came out of the building they found an old ruined cottage nearby. Both buildings were in a hollow and so could not be seen by anyone on the cliff unless they were very close. Jim, judging by the age and state of the buildings, dated the smugglers to the late eighteenth or early nineteenth century. They looked around inside the cottage but couldn't find anything relating to smuggling, except for more old brandy kegs in the cellar. The three lads, their imagination set off, pretended they were the famous smugglers Harry and John Carter (the Prussian King), or Captain Will Richards. They lumbered the old brandy kegs to and fro, from building to cottage, as if they were booty. Margery however didn't join in – she just laughed at them. When the lads were tired of their game they closed over the hole to the tunnel and all of them set off back to camp. When they got there they realised they were really quite dirty, and that the best way of cleaning themselves off was to go for a swim.

That night they slept unusually well.

Falmouth harbour race

ONE EVENING at the beginning of August George Rowe approached Sandy and asked him if he would consider entering the Falmouth harbour race for the under-sixteen boys. The race was run in September. Sandy said he would, but would have to check with his father, as he may be needed on the farm, it being a busy time with the harvest. His father had no objections, and anyway saw it as a good test of his swimming. As to the harvest, the barley and oats would not present insuperable problems without him. He even suggested that if Sandy didn't find this too embarrassing, all the family could come and watch.

On his next training evening Sandy asked if he could take a practice swim across the harbour, in order to gauge the distance and get a feeling for how choppy the water could be. Rowe thought that a tremendous idea, and took him himself the following week. From the vantage of Custom House Quay, he showed him where the race started and finished, but chose a quieter part of the harbour for Sandy to swim across (where the race was actually run was greater in distance and the water was rougher). Sandy said that the water was colder than at Gyllyngvase beach. When he had dried himself off and changed, Rowe told him more about the race. The swimmers would start from large rafts that had been set afloat on the water, and would finish in much the same way on the other side of the harbour. Not apparently concerned, Sandy thanked him and walked the two miles home, pleased with his evening's workout.

When he got in he could hear voices in the parlour. All the family were there, apart from Freddie, who had been put to bed earlier. He told them about his practice session, to which his father replied that it must have been a harder swim than the ones he did at Gyllyngvase. He added that as all the family really wanted to see the race, they were going to have the day off, and after a picnic on the moor continue on to Falmouth. It was important therefore to keep his training up, but with Jim needed by his father for boat repairs, and Margery and Tom on holiday in Redruth, there was plenty of opportunity for that.

Early in September Sandy was needed to help harvest the barley and oats. There was a certain novelty value in that, because this year his father had bought a harvester, a device that was pulled along by two horses. It was much more efficient than hand tools. Despite that, the stalks still had to be bound manually and put in sheaves and stacked in the fields. It was these latter jobs that Sandy was employed to do, which left his back sore and his legs aching. However, his evenings of swimming soon eased those pains away.

He had now been given a date for the race – the second Saturday in September. This was a week after the end of harvesting. To prepare for it, Rowe changed Sandy's training schedule so that he was swimming longer distances. He also taught him how to conserve his strength, in order to sprint over the last twenty or thirty yards of the race. When race day came, they picnicked on the moor as arranged, with Sandy of course eating very little. Thereafter Sandy went on ahead with his father to the starter's hut, which was just on the harbour wall. There they met George Rowe, who registered him for the race. Sandy went and changed.

Before the race started, the rest of Sandy's family arrived. His father found a place to tether the horse and afterwards chose a good vantage point, where everyone could see. A fair crowd had gathered. At two o'clock the ten swimmers in the boys' under-sixteens lined up on the starting raft. When the whistle blew Sandy for some reason hesitated, and was last to dive in the water. He didn't let that bother him, and he didn't rush to catch up. Instead he swam with a steady and powerful stroke, and after about thirty or forty yards had caught up and passed four of those ahead of him. In due course he passed another four, so that now there was only one swimmer ahead of him – Peter Yeo, who also trained at Gyllyngvase. Peter had set off at a pace, but to keep in the lead had over-stretched himself. With fifty yards to go he was only two yards ahead, and starting to tire. This was the right moment for Sandy to start his sprint, and slowly he began to catch up. Under pressure, Peter tired even more, with his strokes becoming irregular and veering to the left. This allowed Sandy to keep swimming straight towards the finishing raft. The crowd was shouting – urging both swimmers on – but by the time Peter had corrected his strokes, Sandy had passed him. From then on he couldn't be caught, and he touched the raft a couple of yards ahead of his rival.

When Sandy and Peter had climbed out of the water they shook each other's hands. The official on the raft congratulated both on their performance. They walked back to the hut at the start, with the crowd cheering, none more loudly than Sandy's family – especially with the presentation of medals – his the winner's, Peter's the runner's-up. George Rowe, who was one of the race officials, congratulated them both. Aside he said to Sandy that all his hard work at the swimming club, plus his exercises during the winter, had made the vital difference. Sandy's family also came to the hut and offered their congratulations. They were quite taken with the medal, and with the prize he received.

Reward for the smugglers' hoard

WHEN THE four friends were trying to plan their trips for the autumn, Sandy had some good news for them. His father, who some time ago had handed in the hoard of gold and silver coins to Customs and Excise, had decided to make some enquiries about a possible reward. At the Customs and Excise office, he was ushered inside and introduced to the supervisor, who unlocked a cabinet and produced an official document. John was asked to read it, and, if he was satisfied with the reward, to sign it. John did, and the reward was £20. The supervisor wished him good day, and after shaking his hand showed him to the door.

John had already decided to share out the money between the four friends. When they heard about this, they were naturally very excited – £20 being riches beyond their wildest dreams. Tom said he'd buy some expensive books on mining engineering. Jim said he would get a set of instruments for use in a drawing office. This was because he expected to work in his father's boat-building firm when he left school. Margery said that she would try to persuade her mother to visit Plymouth, so that she could shop for some good-quality clothes. Sandy had decided that he would buy books on travel, as he still had that itch to see the world.

To such an extent had all this talk preoccupied them that they hadn't decided on their autumn trips. That would have to wait until next Saturday.

Visit to Falmouth to see the fishing fleet

WHEN NEXT Saturday came, they did initially talk about their plans, but soon got on to the topic of spending their rewards. The lads' parents had agreed with their proposals, as long as their fathers went along with them to advise before they made their purchases. Margery said her mother was at first reluctant to take her to Plymouth, but after some persuasion had given in to her request — and even arranged for them to stay with a cousin there.

When they turned their attentions again to their autumn outings, Jim made the best suggestion. They should take a trip in the pony and trap to Falmouth, the reason being that with the weather so stormy the fishing fleet tied up at port was sure to be a sight to behold. As no one had any better ideas, this is what they agreed to do. Sure enough, when they got there, and looked along the harbour wall, they were amazed to see so many large fishing boats berthed at the quayside or anchored close by. They found it remarkable that all the vessels they saw were clean and tidy, with ropes gathered and stowed neatly on the decks, and the brasses on all the equipment polished and gleaming. On some of the boats the crews were washing down the decks. At the quayside there were fishermen mending their nets, some of which had been badly torn in the storms.

Jim pointed out vessels that he knew from his fishing trips. He stopped at one, because he knew the captain. 'Good morning,' he shouted out. Captain Pearce recognised him at once, and invited him and his friends on board. He took them into his cabin and drew up benches for them to sit. He called out to one of his crew members, who doubled as the cook, telling him to bring up from the galley something to drink and some cake. 'How's your father getting along, Jim?' he said. He hadn't seen him since he'd carried out some repairs about a year ago. Jim replied that his father was *always* busy, and more so with the extra work taken on at Porth Navas, as well as in Falmouth. Sandy asked the captain how his fishing boat had fared in the storm. The captain replied that luckily the crew had an early catch of fish and had been making their way back and were close to Falmouth when the storm broke, so the vessel hadn't been damaged. By contrast many of the other boats had been caught and had lost their nets. Others had broken masts or damage shipsides. Sandy could imagine the tall masts splintering and the crack of the wooden planks as huge waves hit the fishing boats.

The captain said he knew Sandy's father from when he owned his joiner's shop in Falmouth. He had heard he'd inherited a farm from his uncle. He asked Sandy how he liked being on a farm, to which he replied that although at times the work was hard he enjoyed the freedom of the countryside. It was great too to be able to meet up with his friends and go out on trips together. The captain gave them a tour of the boat before escorting them to the gangway. They thanked him for his hospitality. Now they could begin to see, as they walked along the quay, damage that many of the other fishing boats had suffered. One of them had badly split planks.

They continued to marvel at so many fishing vessels, for never had they seen so many in Falmouth at one time. They walked back along the quayside, and after looking back briefly set off home. It was doubtful they would be able to meet again for a couple of weeks, what with the lifting of the potato crop and other vegetables, and so much repair work to be done on ships at the harbour. But they would get together again as soon as they could.

Margery and her mother visit Plymouth

GOOD AUTUMN weather saw the harvest completed much more quickly than anticipated, which was just the opportunity for Margery and her mother to make their visit to Plymouth. The latter had written to her cousin – who lived there – at the beginning of October, asking if they could stay. She had had a positive response. So, they packed enough clothes for the weekend, and left Falmouth by train on the Friday afternoon, Margery having finished school early at midday. For her the journey through Cornwall was an adventure, because she'd never travelled far from home before. Her mother pointed out all the famous landmarks, and when they crossed the bridge over the Tamar she explained that its intricate structure had been designed by the famous English engineer, Isambard Kingdom Brunel.

They arrived at Plymouth's North Road Station in the early evening, where they were met by Mrs Richards' cousin (married name, Rodgers). She had hired a hackney carriage from a firm called Cadell, and once the luggage was on board the three of them were driven up to the Rodgers' house near the Hoe. There they had a hot meal, and afterwards went out for a look around. They strolled in the part of the Hoe where Francis Drake had played bowls before commanding his ships to defeat the Spanish Armada. Then they took in the citadel, the fortress made famous in the civil war between Cromwell's army and the royalists. From there they went on to the Barbican, where Margery and her mother were shown where the Pilgrim Fathers had set out for North America. After looking in the shops they stopped at a ships' chandler's, which was open, where out of curiosity Margery looked in through the open door of the workshop. She could see two men working in there, the place suffused with the smell of tarred rope and resin. The two men were splicing and dressing rope, in a rhythmic beat of mallets.

Next morning the three of them rose early and after breakfast walked from the Rodgers' house in The Crescent to the Guildhall, whose limestone walls were all a-glisten after rain in the night. Outside the Guildhall was the grave of Captain Bligh, of the ship the *Bounty*, famous for its mutinous crew in 1789. From there they went on to the shop of Messrs J Hepworth and Son in Bedford Street, though could find nothing suitable there to buy – clothes *or* material. As the bookseller Bazley and Co was in the same street they went in there next. After browsing round Margery found what she wanted – two books on animal husbandry, because of her interest in the care of farm animals. However, as the main purpose of their shopping expedition was clothes for Margery, to be paid for out of her reward money, they moved on to George Street. There they went into J B Moulder's shop, a tailor and outfitter who specialised in ladies' clothes. Almost at once Margery found a dress that she liked. It had been especially made for a particular customer, who had changed her mind about buying it. Margery tried it on and it fitted her well. Her mother saw how suitable it was and bought it, then examined some of the materials for making up dresses and jackets. She selected some lengths of cloth and accessories to match, and these she also bought, together with some hats they liked. For all three of them it was a very satisfactory shopping outing.

When they got home Mr Rodgers, who had just returned from a business trip to London, said his hellos and offered to take them on a trip round Plymouth. He brought his horse and trap up to the front door, and when they were all seated he drove off with gusto. First he took them to the town centre, then to Millbay Docks, where the fishing boats landed their catches. After that he drove on to Devonport, past the high stone walls enclosing the royal dockyard, where Royal Navy warships were built and refitted. Then he turned into Wolseley Road, where they stopped and visited friends of the Rodgers and had tea. From here Margery and her mother could see the famous bridge over the Tamar. When they had had their tea and said goodbye they were driven back to Plymouth via Wolseley and Alma Roads, to George Street. As it was now evening it was here that Mr Rodgers stopped, to let Margery and her mother see the gas jets lighting up the shop windows. Later, when they were having their evening meal, Margery asked what the different names Devonport, Stonehouse and Plymouth represented. He explained that these were the original three towns, but with their expansion over the years they had become so inter-linked that they were now more or less one. Next day after breakfast they said their farewells, inviting Mr and Mrs Rodgers to visit the farm soon. Mr Rodgers drove them to the station. As they settled in their seats, they were surprised to see William Minhinick (father of the boy saved by Sandy) and his eldest son George enter the compartment. Mrs Richards knew Minhinick, as he owned several farms near their own, and as with John Toye rented them land.

Minhinick introduced his son. George was about sixteen, had fair hair, fine features, and was tall. Being younger, Margery knew of him only from comments her brother had made, he and Tom being at the same school. Minhinick said he'd had business in Plymouth, and had brought his son for the experience. They'd taken the opportunity to spend the weekend there, and see all the sights. George was very easy-going, and was soon in conversation with Margery. He noticed the books she'd bought, and so the two of them were soon discussing their mutual interest in the care and development of good farm stock. By the time they reached Falmouth, Mr Richards was at the station waiting, as was Mrs Minhinick. There were further introductions between the two families before they all set off respectively for home. As they were all driving away, George shouted out to Margery that he hoped to see her at the fireworks display on the 5th of November at the Bonallack mansion. Margery surprised herself at her own reply. She would be there with friends, she said, and looked forward to seeing him. Mr Richards gave a knowing nod to his wife.

Halloween and the fireworks display

THE FOUR friends when they met up at the old barn on the following Saturday exchanged stories, Margery revelling in her trip to Plymouth, and Sandy recounting his win at the harbour race. He showed them his medal and prize. For his part, Jim had been involved in the repair of a luxury yacht, a commission his father had taken on at Porth Navas in the last couple of months. It was an extensive repair, as the yacht had run aground on rocks near Porthoustock. The unusual cabin fittings he described in graphic detail, to the point that the others couldn't wait to see the yacht. 'I'll arrange it,' he said. The repair would be complete, he thought, in about two weeks' time, and they could visit it while it was still on the slip. This would be the weekend after Halloween and the fireworks display at the mansion house. If they could get time off from their farm work, then there was no reason why they shouldn't stay at Porth Navas, because his father had converted part of the workshop into a bunkhouse and mess room. Originally this had been for the additional workmen employed on a wide range of repairs, when so many vessels had been damaged in the storms off Falmouth. 'I'll ask my dad,' Jim said, 'if we're allowed.'

In the meantime the Toyes and the Richards family prepared for the Halloween party. This year it was going to be held at the Richards'. Margery and Tom prepared the games and their mother the food, including cakes and sweetmeats. Freddie and Sandy went as ghosts, while Margery was a gypsy and Tom a pirate. There were the usual games, and these were played at a frantic pace. Freddie won most of them, as he was nimbler than the others. When the games needed music, Margery's mother played the piano – though she did find it hard to keep up with musical chairs without dissolving into laughter, what with the antics of the players. Often when the music stopped they ended up in a heap on the floor, with the vacated chairs still vacant. Sandy's mother and father and brother Joe dropped in just as the games finished, whereupon the two families sat down and enjoyed an excellent meal.

When it was time for the Toyes to go home, Freddie was the very picture of contentment, a boy with a full stomach and cream still smeared on his face. He clutched at his prizes, but being very tired was tucked up in bed as soon as they got home. The rest of them chatted in the parlour until it was time for them to retire.

During the next few days preparations for the firework display were made at the Bonallack mansion. This year there were going to be many more wooden structures to enhance the display. When, duly, the evening came round, Jim came out to drive them over in his pony and cart. However, just as they were leaving the Richards' farm to go down the hill a barn door slammed and the noise frightened the pony. Out of control, it galloped down the hill, at such speed that the cart swung from side to side. The friends didn't know if the cart would hit the hedge or overturn. Each time the wheels hit a large stone it bucked and bounced out of control. The ordeal seemed endless, but, nevertheless, Jim managed to regain control and bring them to a stop at the bottom of the hill. He climbed out, and talking to the pony softly, sometimes in a whisper, managed to calm him down. Satisfied that no one was badly injured, beyond a sore rib or two and a few bruises here and there, they set off on their journey again – at as leisurely a pace as possible.

A good crowd had already gathered when they arrived, and the bonfire blazed merrily. Jim found a safe spot to tether the pony, and they found themselves a suitable place to view. After a few minutes, Margery looked about to see who else was there. George Minhinick was nearby with his friends and she gave him a wave. He came over and said how pleased he was to see her again. Embarrassed slightly, she introduced him to her brother and other two friends. George said he'd heard Sandy's name mentioned by his father, who had been nothing but full of praise for how he had saved John from drowning. This time it was Sandy's turn to feel embarrassment, and he replied that what he'd done was a mere nothing. Everyone there had been trained as life-savers, and it just happened to be him who was swimming nearby. George chatted to Margery a little longer, and had a brief exchange of views with Tom, before returning to his own friends. Then in a few minutes the display started, with the fireworks weaving their tapestries of coloured fire on the frameworks constructed for them. The display ended with large rockets zooming up into the vault of the sky, before exploding in a cascade of coloured sparks. When it was time for the friends to go, Margery waved goodbye to George.

This time Jim drove very carefully, not wanting a repeat of earlier events, and happily all arrived home safely. Next outing was Porth Navas, and the bunkhouse.

A weekend at Porth Navas

SANDY'S MOTHER prepared him his food, including Cornish pasties, and Margery did the same for herself and Tom. Then Sandy packed his bags, and slinging them over his shoulder made his way up to the Richards' place. At six o'clock sharp Jim arrived with his pony and cart, and soon after that they were off. On the way there, Jim was endlessly quizzed as to what the bunkhouse was like. 'It's marvellous,' he said. 'But you'll have to wait and see.'

It didn't take them long to get there. At the slip they could see the yacht perched high on its blocks, ready for launch. As the bunkhouse and workshop were serviced by separate doors, they were able to load their things in without encroaching on the workspace. They were pleasantly surprised at the size of the bunkhouse. It had a large dining area with a small kitchen at the end, and next to that was a small room with two beds and a lot of cupboard space. This went back to the time when Jim's father and supervisor had a large number of workmen employed on the slip and in the workshop. Adjacent to this room was another, much larger one, with more bunk beds and cupboard space. Margery had the small room, and the three lads the larger one. Pretty soon they'd all settled in and were busy with their evening meal.

As usual Jim had brought fish to cook. Sandy prepared and boiled vegetables he had brought from the farm, and heated the pasties in an oven, which was roaring away with sticks and coal (courtesy Jim). Margery and Tom set out cutlery and plates. From what they'd brought with them they provided some very attractive additions in the shape of ham and other cold meats, and pickled vegetables. Margery added the final touches with fruit and cakes. They ate heartily, and over their meal discussed what they would do the following day. Jim suggested that after looking round the yacht they could go down to the River Helford and collect oysters, where you could find them in shallow waters.

They rose early the next day, and after a hasty breakfast went out to the slip. The yacht's hull had a light blue coat, and the upper parts were white. The brass fittings on the deck and cabin sparkled in the sunshine. Most impressive, however, was the sheer size and finish of the yacht. Jim said his father had worked hard at the repair (and Jim himself had helped), and had even employed specialist painters to restore it to its former glory. Suitably awed, they returned to the bunkhouse and prepared their trip to the river. The walk there was over rough ground and so would take some time, and for that reason they decided to take a picnic. Before leaving Jim picked up two hammers and land-cutters (these latter were thin-bladed chisels, used for cutting away planks on wooden boats, but ideal for prising oysters off the rocks). November it might be, but the weather was fine, and after a pleasant half-hour walk they arrived at the headland above the river. To reach the oyster bed they had to pass around the headland, where there was a sheltered rocky spot where the water was shallow. They took off their boots and stockings, then waded into the water – cold but bearable. Then they began their work, knocking off or prising free the oyster shells. Margery collected them and stowed them in a bag.

Presently it was time for their picnic. They sat down on the bank and dried their feet and legs before emptying out their bags, and tucked in with aplomb. While they chattered Tom hushed all the others, saying he could hear a baby crying in the distance. 'That's not a baby,' said Jim. 'That's seals you can hear, further along the river.'

'Oh, let's go and have a look then,' Margery said.

'All right,' said Jim. 'I'll show you where they bask on the rocks.'

He led them along the bank to a rocky inlet partly hidden in a bend in the river. As they climbed over a land-rise they could see five or six seals sunning themselves on the rocks, so here they stopped, and watched for a good long while, spellbound.

On their way back to the bunkhouse Jim could see his father working on a whaling boat. He had cut out a good number of planks on both sides the previous day, and was now preparing new ones. Jim asked him why his shipwright hadn't turned up for work. 'He's ill,' he said. He'd had a message the previous evening. Sandy and Tom asked if they could help. Although they hadn't done any boat work before, they'd laboured for their fathers on timber repairs to barns and fences. As they seemed so keen, Jim and Margery felt obliged to offer their help too.

'You're on!' Jim's father said. The best way they could help was to load the new planks into the steam kiln. Once they were sufficiently steamed they could be brought out one by one to the whaler, where he and Jim would fit and clamp them in place, while they were still hot and supple. As the joints had already been scarfed, once the planks were in the kiln all that was needed was the fire stoked and kiln steaming. While that was taking place, the four friends returned to the bunkhouse for a drink. Jim's father fetched his tools, some copper nails and clamps, and canvas gloves for handling the planks from the kiln. As each one came out, they had to run it to the whaler before it cooled down. Jim and his father fitted, clamped and drilled the planks, before driving in the nails. For the planks to keep their shape while they went through this process, the nails were fitted with roes and clenched. Also the scarfs at the plank ends were secured with small copper nails clenched into the planks.

Sandy, Tom and Margery also helped with the riveting. Taking it in turns they supported the nail-heads with steel dollies, while Jim and his father fitted roes over them inside the boat. They then cut the nails to a suitable length and clenched them over the roes. It was hot and dirty work, and by the time the riveting was finished the three were smeared in grime and sweat: Tom, Sandy and Margery looked like chimney sweeps. The other two roared with laughter. The three went into the bunkhouse and saw for themselves in the mirror how comic it looked, and laughed at it themselves.

Jim's father soaked the new whaler planks with water, so that the timber would swell and make the joins watertight. When the others had finished washing, he came into the bunkhouse and thanked them for all their help. He said that he couldn't stay as he'd work to finish at home. Before he left he said he had left fresh bread and cakes in the kitchen, which his wife had baked for them. With the oysters, and what they had left over, it was all very palatable. They tucked in as if there was no tomorrow, and were soon full and exhausted and ready for bed.

When they returned home next day, they said they would like to arrange something similar again. 'Next spring,' said Jim, 'when the weather's warmer.'

The farmhouse damaged by the storm

THE WEATHER over the next few weeks got colder and wetter, and so the four friends didn't meet so often. On Saturdays Sandy would go up to the Richards' farm from time to time, while Jim visited only once since the weekend at the bunkhouse – and that was to tell Tom and Margery he'd be busy helping his father with boat repairs.

Sandy's home life was mainly centred on the dairy, and with helping his father collect and store enough fodder to last the animals through the winter. His mother was again busy in the kitchen preserving and storing vegetables and cold meats. Sometimes Sandy helped her.

Come the evenings, when the farm work was done, the family would sit in the parlour, and while Sandy and Freddie were busy with schoolwork, their father and mother would read (Joe preferred to look at books in his own room). On one Friday evening, mid-December, Elizabeth was reading *Jane Eyre*

(Charlotte Brontë), while John was engrossed in Dickens (*A Christmas Carol*). By day it had been getting much windier, with heavy rain. By evening the wind was stronger. Then a storm hit the farmhouse. They could hear the rattle of roof slates, first as they were lifted, then as they cascaded down the roof – and the damage was obviously severe. John went upstairs and looked in the bedrooms for leaks. In Sandy's room water was coming through the ceiling in several places. He shouted down the stairway for someone to bring up buckets, or any other receptacle, which they positioned as best they could. Then they removed mattresses from the beds. With the storm still buffeting the house, it wasn't possible to cover the damage to the roof just yet, but there was a large canvas in one of the barns that they could use when the wind died down. John went out to look for it, while the rest did a job of mopping up. When they were all back in the parlour, John said he'd found a suitable canvas – it had eyelets, through which he could rope it. Weather permitting, he would do that next morning.

When it got late the family went to their beds, very much doubting they would sleep – and that turned out to be the case. Joe and Sandy lay awake in conversation, talking about what they would do when they were older. Sandy said he knew their father wanted him to take over the dairy once he was old enough, and although he didn't want to disappoint him, what he really wanted to do was go to sea. In the last couple of years that was a yearning that only seemed to have intensified. Joe on the other hand enjoyed working with his father, and saw life on a farm as very much healthier than toiling away in a tin mine, or in one of the foundries in Falmouth. He went on to say that he had met a girl called Mary Harvey, who was about his own age. This was at a dance in the village. Her father was a farmer with land near Constantine, and so musing, both of them did finally fall asleep, the wind and the rain still swirling about them outside.

Next morning Sandy's father was up early and got his ropes and canvas together, and started working on the roof. Sandy and Joe hurried through their breakfast and came outside to help, dragging the heavy canvas out of the barn. They fetched two long ladders, and propped them against the house. With Sandy and his mother holding the ladders steady, Joe and his father pulled the canvas up onto the roof and spread it over the damaged area, and from there lowered the ropes, where Sandy lashed them to heavy stones and fence posts. Then they all had a job gathering up the broken slates in the courtyard, and after that collected and emptied the buckets from upstairs. Last job was to move the mattresses and bedding back.

It was not until Monday that the wind died down enough for Sandy's father to work safely on the roof, and make good the temporary repair. He drove over to Falmouth to buy not only slates but also lead sheeting for the flashing round the chimney, which was in need of renewal. On his way back he could see that many other houses had suffered like his, and outside Falmouth itself there were many fallen trees and branches. When his farm hands helped him remove the canvas, he was now ready to make the repair more permanent. Joe helped with the lead and the slates, the latter proving not too troublesome. The flashing round the chimney took a bit of time, however, because the joints between the stack and the roof had to be remade.

By evening, though, John Toye was able to announce to his family that the roof was good and sound – though he wouldn't paint the ceiling in Sandy's room until it had dried out.

The family celebrates Christmas

A FEW days before Christmas, because of the bad weather, Sandy's father had arranged to meet all his farm hands in the large barn. When they were assembled he thanked them for all their hard work during the year and wished them and their families a happy Christmas. He paid them their annual bonuses plus their wages for the holiday period – two weeks including Christmas Eve. It was a time of year when little could be done on the farm, so a break for everyone was always on the cards.

Over the last month or so Joe had been making a model yacht for Freddie's Christmas present. Sandy had got some drawings from Jim Earle, and these enabled Joe to cut the timber to the correct shape. Sandy made the sails from cloth, and for the masts he used some spare wood that his father had in the workshop. Sandy also asked Jim for any spare paint left over from the yacht at Porth Navas. He found two small tins, which he brought to the farm just before Christmas. Joe's father made a keel from tin plate, which he fitted to the yacht before it was painted.

The last few days before Christmas were a busy time for the Toye family, everyone confined to separate rooms wrapping up presents. One special present John had bought for his son Freddie was a model steam engine. This had been manufactured for him by an engineering firm in Falmouth, by a business associate he'd known from the firm for many years.

Come Christmas Eve, Sandy took presents from his own to the Richards family. They too were busy with preparations. Mr Richards was making up a punch, and his wife and Margery were preparing the Christmas feast. Seeing how preoccupied they were, Sandy stayed only a short while, then returned home to his own jobs.

Breakfast was brief on Christmas Day, and after it the Toyes retired to the parlour to unwrap their presents, which had been put there the previous night long after the children had gone to bed. Sandy and Joe had been given books by their father and warm heavy jackets by their mother. Hers were small presents from the boys and a silk shawl from her husband. John had books from his boys and a pipe from his wife (he tended to smoke only in the evenings, when there was time to relax). Freddie unwrapped his smaller presents – games and puzzles mainly. If *they* gave him pleasure, he squeaked with delight. When he unwrapped the two larger gifts, he was taken aback by the sheer size of the yacht. The detail lavished on the steam engine left him agog with joy. Its brass boiler glinted in the morning light, and there was even a whistle that was operated by it. When the two flat candles under the boiler had been alight for a few minutes, the water turned into steam, and that drove the mechanical hammer.

When he'd had some fun with that, Freddie asked his father when they could sail the yacht. He replied they would have to pick a day after Christmas and go to the harbour at Falmouth and sail it there. They'd need a quiet part of the inner harbour, clear of any ships.

With the boys' presents unwrapped and taken to their rooms, it was time for their Christmas meal. To the boys it was quite a feast: cooked chicken, cold meats and steaming hot vegetables for the main course. This was followed by apple pie, jelly and cakes. When they had finished they were so full up that all they wanted was a rest. They recovered a bit by the evening, and John got out his skittles and challenged them to a game. They set them up in the long passageway, and for the next hour all one could hear was the clunk of them being knocked down, and shouts from the excitable players. After that, it was time for some light refreshment again.

As it was now late in the evening, Freddie – after much protest – was put to bed, while Sandy, Joe and their parents retired to the parlour. After an hour or so they all felt the ill effects of over-eating, and they moaned as they climbed upstairs to their beds.

The weather deteriorated during the next week, with rain most days, and so Freddie had to wait until the start of the new year before he was able to sail his yacht. The first Saturday after New Year's was good, however, so they took a trip to the harbour and for the first time Freddie could see his yacht afloat. Joe and Sandy were keen to come along too, as they had built the sail. As ever, their mother made them a hamper. As it was still on the cold side, all the family wrapped up warm, with Sandy and Joe in their new heavy jackets. They stopped at a spot just above a shingle beach that sloped down to the water, where Freddie could proudly carry his yacht to the water-line and back. Joe tied a long piece of cord to the stern, in case it drifted too far out into the harbour. When Freddie put his yacht in the water and pushed it off the breeze caught the sails and took it out from the beach. But the workmanship was good, and the yacht stayed upright with the keel straight and steady in the water. Freddie was overjoyed. The breeze caught the sails again and took it well away from the shore, with Joe holding it back with the cord. Freddie said it looked like a real yacht at sea, if you looked at it through half-closed eyes. His brothers humoured him, much to their parents' amusement.

For a picnic treat they followed up their pasties with something very special – buns filled with clotted cream. As was his wont, Freddie ended up with nearly as much cream on his face as in his stomach. It turned much colder shortly after that, so it wasn't long before they were packing up and on their way home.

A day out in Falmouth

AFTER A hard week digging up the root crops and taking them to Falmouth for sale, Sandy's father decided he would take a

Saturday off, and treat his wife to a day out in Falmouth. As he had made much more from his sale than expected, he told her she could visit the dressmaker and buy some spring and summer clothes. On the Friday before, Sandy and Joe were told of the plan, and that their parents wouldn't return until after a hotel dinner. Sandy had to do his milk deliveries, and Joe had to look after Freddie and make sure he went to bed at the proper time. These instructions clear, John and his wife set off in the horse and trap, reaching Falmouth at about ten o'clock on the Saturday morning. After stabling the horse near the town centre, they made their way to the shops. The first dressmaker they visited didn't have much in stock, so they found another, where Elizabeth bought a dress she liked. She also looked at materials, choosing a cloth from which she could make a jacket and skirt. As measuring up was going to take some time, John went to a nearby tailor's, where he wanted to buy a waistcoat. When he'd got the one he wanted, he returned to the dressmaker, where Elizabeth was sitting down and talking to the proprietress. They were discussing a date for the final fitting.

John hurried her up, and from here they strolled to the Falmouth Hotel in Melville Road. There they ordered coffee and sat down in the lounge. After a few minutes the hotel proprietor, a Mr Watten, came to greet them. He welcomed them warmly as he knew John from work he had carried out at the hotel as a joiner. After coffee they walked round the hotel grounds – almost four acres, and overlooking the bay. They stopped to admire the sea view, the Castle Sands below, and on a headland Pendennis Castle itself. Then they made their way back to the hotel for an early lunch – soup and a main course piping hot. After lunch, John wanted to visit their friend George Tucker, whose family lived in Killigrew Street, not far from where the Toyes used to be. Since moving to the farm John had met up with George only on his visits to the market.

George and his wife Mary had two children, a son also called George, who was twenty and worked in a foundry, and a daughter Alice, who was two years younger, and worked as a clerk in a solicitor's office. George was self-employed as a plumber. He said they were lucky to find him in, because at the moment, with so many winter emergencies, he was being called out a lot – burst pipes mainly. By chance today was slack and he was doing his accounts. The old friends chatted and drank tea into the early evening, until it was time for the Toyes to head back to the hotel for dinner. 'You must come and visit us on the farm,' said John.

'Be delighted,' said George.

'We'll arrange it next market day.'

They went back to the hotel, where a sumptuous dinner with all the trimmings awaited, which to Elizabeth was sheer luxury.

When they had finished their coffee John said he'd collect the horse and trap and bring it round to the hotel. Mr Watten chatted away to Elizabeth, and helped her up when John had driven round. 'Safe journey,' he said. 'Do visit again soon.' Little did he know that a 'safe journey' wasn't to be granted.

John drove out to the road home, and for the first half-mile the journey went well. Then they felt a wobble in one of the wheels. John climbed down and saw that it was loose, though finding a large stone he managed to force it back into place on the axle. For the next mile their journey was stop-start, the wheel having to be knocked back in place repeatedly, so that his coat and shirt got covered in grease. His face was streaked with dirt. Finally, with only half a mile to drive, the wheel jammed itself on the axle at a steep angle to the road. John climbed out and tried to hammer it back again, though this time it wouldn't budge an inch – no matter how hard he tried. After a last kick – more in frustration than anything else – he told his wife they would have to release the horse and ride it home. So, unhitching Blackie, that is precisely what they did.

Meanwhile Joe had made sure that Freddie had got to bed at a reasonable hour, despite his protests, and he and Sandy tidied up the kitchen. As time went on they got a bit anxious, with still no sign of their parents. They looked out for them, to-ing and fro-ing between the hearth and window repeatedly – and still the horse and trap failed to appear. They did however eventually hear the horse's hoofs. This was a puzzle, until they could see clearly Blackie at the entrance of the courtyard, their mother and father mounted atop and looking quite perplexed. Bareback wasn't the best means of travel. Their mother was calm, but their father was less than happy, and dishevelled to boot.

The two lads dared not say anything, knowing that their father was likely to lose his temper if he saw them laugh. He told them in the strongest terms that first thing tomorrow they'd be needed to help him repair the trap. Sandy and Joe waited until both their parents had gone up to bed, then quietly closed the door on themselves in the kitchen and guffawed without restraint. What a sight their dad had been, bareback on his horse, and covered in dirt and grease!

Next morning John called the two boys down to an early breakfast, then fetched out Blackie and one other horse from the stable, and putting halters on both attached them to the wagon, Blackie to pull, the other harnessed behind. Sandy and Joe fetched tools, some wedges and some lengths of timber. Then they set off for the abandoned trap. When they got there they lifted the wheel free of the ground, which allowed them to support the axle with the timbers they'd brought. After much effort Joe and his father managed to pull the wheel free, then gradually eased it back to its normal position. Joe holding it in place, his father drove the wedges into the gaps between the wheel and axle, so securing it but allowing it to rotate. Joe and Sandy then loaded up the wagon while their father harnessed Blackie to the trap, which was driven back slowly, lest its wheel came loose again. On the following Monday John set off for the local blacksmith, where the repair was made more permanent.

Fortunately it had all been so very minor, as accidents go. Next month a more serious one occurred, and befell the Richards family.

Mrs Richards has a serious accident

IT HAPPENED at the beginning of March, and was a bolt from the blue. On market day Mrs Richards had driven the wagon to Falmouth to stock up with provisions, and had taken much longer than expected. To make up for the delay she drove hard and very fast on the journey back home. Most of the way all went well, and she made good time. However, when she reached the heavily rutted road about a mile from the farm, she didn't drop her pace. About a hundred yards on one of the wheels struck a large stone. The wagon lurched on its side and toppled into the ditch. She was thrown off and fell awkwardly on her side. Her wrist snapped, and there was a numbing ache to one of her legs. In fact the pain was so extreme she passed out.

After how long she didn't know, but she recovered consciousness, and saw that the horse hadn't been hit by the wagon, and had managed to stand up. Then she heard a shout from along the road. Sandy's father and one of his hands were returning from Falmouth and saw the horse and the overturned wagon. John could see Mrs Richards lying in the ditch, and that her face was covered in blood. He pulled up near and jumped from his seat and tried to see how bad her injuries were. He could tell that her wrist was broken, and that her left side had borne the brunt of the fall. He and his farm hand lifted her carefully on to the wagon, then John told him to carry on up to the Richards' farm to tell them he was taking her to hospital. At the hospital, two porters wheeled her on a trolley to theatre. When a doctor came, he gave her a sedative, then carried out his examination. Not only was her wrist broken, she had a break to her ankle. Nurses came in and cleaned her up, then she was moved to an operating table, where the doctor administered chloroform. After that had taken effect, he reset the wrist and ankle bones, and put them in plaster.

Other than facial scratches, and bruising to her side, there were no other problems. One of the nurses cleaned up her face and treated the bruises on her side. Then she was moved to a bed in the main ward. In the evening both the Toyes and the Richards family came to visit. They were allowed to see her for only a short while as she was still woozy with the pain and anaesthetic. She would need several days in hospital to recover, and once home would need many weeks of rest before the plaster came off and the bruising healed. Over the next three or four days she had many more visitors – from not only her family and neighbours, but from friends in Falmouth and other farms too. Even her relations from Redruth came.

After about five days she was allowed to go home, her husband collecting her in their horse and trap. She had to use crutches to walk, and needed his help climbing to the seat. Mr Richards drove with a great deal of caution, as you'd imagine, and when they got home there were Margery and Tom as well as the Toyes with an emotional welcome.

For the next six weeks the four friends didn't see each other quite so often, as Margery and Tom not only had their farm work, but also a lot of extra tasks with their mother incapacitated as she was. After a further six weeks the casts were removed, though Mrs Richards still had to use a stick to get about the place. For another month she had to put her foot up and rest for several hours each day.

The four friends leave school

MARCH AND April of 1891 were a decisive period for the four friends. Margery left school in the first of those months, and was at home taking care of her mother, running the farmhouse, and generally seeing to most domestic matters. Sandy left school in April, as he was now fourteen and his father needed him to take over the dairy. His mother hadn't been well recently and had been told by her doctor to rest. Tom and Jim, who were both fifteen, left in April too, and took up the careers arranged by their fathers. Tom had been accepted as an engineering apprentice, and would serve his time at a mine near Redruth. His uncle, who deputised for the captain of the mine, Tom now lived with. To get his engineering qualifications, he had days out at the Camborne School of Mining. Jim, as had always been expected, started as apprentice shipwright in his father's boat-building yard at Falmouth. Part of that apprenticeship involved training in the yard's drawing office.

With so complete a change to their lives the four friends would not have the same opportunities to see each other, but on their last meeting in the barn were determined to meet and arrange at least *some* trips, however infrequent.

With a late completion to the ploughing, due to a blizzard that struck most of Cornwall on and after the 9th of March, Sandy was kept horrendously busy. As well as looking after the dairy he had to help clear the fields. Then with the heavy falls of snow Joe, Sandy and their father – as well as the farm hands – had to spend several days making the farm roads passable. The freak conditions had been the worst experienced in Cornwall during that century.

With the ploughing over at last, Sandy was left with just the dairy, which gave him free time in the evenings. Sometimes he walked up the hill to the Richards' place, to see how Mrs Richards was recovering from her injuries. Although Margery was nearly always busy when he came, she nevertheless stopped her work and made time to sit with him and chew the fat. On other evenings he walked down to Falmouth harbour, and there watched the ships sailing in or out. He often wished he was on a ship about to sail away, and he still had that yearning for faraway places. Some of the seamen got to know him by sight, and would often nod or wave. Their faces all seemed etched with the rigours of life at sea, their complexions badly marked or ravaged by cold winds or poor diet. One he always saw had white hair but a young face, with a scar that ran the length of his cheek, deep and livid. He was stocky, muscular, barrel-chested, and his naked arms showed flesh like leather. His hands were blistered, with two fingers missing.

He told Sandy his name was Will Pearce, and that he hailed originally from Penzance. He had sailed on various ships over the last twenty years, from large cargo vessels to smaller fishing boats. They began to meet often, and Will would tell him stories about his voyages. One evening Sandy asked him about his injuries. Will explained that once on a cargo ship they were hit by a storm. Some of the deck cargo broke loose, and in trying to move it the winch jammed and the wire snapped, catching his hand and slashing his face. He was lucky, he said, not to have been more badly injured, what with the hawser whipping along the deck. Tragic as it was, his story didn't deter Sandy from wanting to go to sea.

On evenings when the weather was poor, rather than go to the harbour, or visit the Richards' place, he would sometimes help his mother in the kitchen. He even began to cook some of the evening meals.

Sandy and Joe's visit to a boat-building yard

ONE EVENING at the end of April, just as the Toye family finished their evening meal, there was a loud knock at the door. John went to see, and there at the doorstep was his cousin Robert. They shook hands warmly, and Robert Toye was ushered in and shown a seat by the fire. He explained why he'd come. He told them he had had some business in Constantine, and he was calling in on his way home to Falmouth. He apologised for not having seen them for over a year, but he had been extremely busy with his fishing business, planning and building a new boat. It was now under construction at a boat builder's in Falmouth, so he wondered whether John's older sons would like to see it. Sandy and Joe said they would.

'That's handsome of you,' John said. 'How about if I bring them over next Saturday, because as a matter of fact I've got some business in Falmouth myself...'

'That sounds grand,' Robert said. 'Ten o'clock do you?'

'Ten o'clock sounds fine.'

'And we really must meet up more often.'

'I couldn't agree more.'

On Saturday morning Sandy and Joe were up promptly and making their preparations. Their father still had some work to do on the farm, but would have them in Falmouth by ten. Indeed they made good time, and were met by Robert at the entrance to the yard. The two cousins chatted for a while, then John left his sons there and drove into town, where there were things he needed to do. Robert led the two lads round the yard, with its timber stacks left to season, and other piles ready for the sawmill – lengths of elm, oak, and mahogany. They actually went to the mill to see some timbers as they were being cut, where the noise from not only the steam engine, but also the pulleys that worked the saws, was deafening. They covered their ears. The smell though of cut wood was not unpleasant.

After the mill they were shown into the office, which with its broad windows was light and airy, ideal for the draughtsmen working there. These latter were young, perhaps in their early twenties. They smiled and proffered a cheery good day. They were working, Robert said, on plans for another fishing boat, for a firm in Penzance. He showed them to another bench, where there were drawings for his own fishing boat. They were design drawings, he said, done to scale, encompassing the sheer, body and half-breadth plans, showing dimensions and shape in different planes. Robert explained that details from these plans were transferred to larger scale drawings, so that the lines of the boat in various views could be faired, so giving the vessel its smooth curvature. By taking distances from these plans measurements were transferred to a large scrieve board, made up of butted, painted planks, and lines were cut permanently into the wood. This allowed the curvature and full-scale measurements relating to different parts of the structure to be transferred to wooden moulds. From these moulds the boat's timbers were cut and shaped.

They went back to the main building, where he showed them the scrieve board, where the faired lines of his fishing boat had been cut into the painted surface. 'Hope this is not all too complicated,' Robert said. Sandy and Joe replied that they understood the general principles.

Close to the side of the building were some wooden benches, at these two craftsmen – shipwrights by trade – were working on fishing-boat timbers, either new or under repair. One of them was cutting out a boat's knee, while another was shaping part of a stem. Others were preparing main frames for erection on a fishing boat, which was at an early stage of its build on one of the slips. Hanging on the wall behind them were the tools of their trade – saws, chisels, mallets, wooden planes, spokeshaves, clamps – all arranged tidily for easy access.

They ventured out to the slips, where the fishing boats they saw were all at different stages. Joe asked why they all had different types of planking. 'Some,' Robert said, 'are clinker build.' That meant the hull was constructed with each plank overlapping the one below. They were bound together on the frames by copper nails clenched over copper roves. 'The other type of build is called carvel.' That was where the inner planks were set diagonally and the outer horizontally. Again copper nails were clenched on copper roves. Seams at the outer planks were caulked with oakum strands, and that made the hull watertight. 'My own boat,' he said, 'is carvel. The planking's much thicker and more strongly secured than clinker.' This design of hull planking would withstand more wear and tear than boats of clinkerbuild that mainly fished in coastal waters.

They went to the slip where Robert's partly built boat was. Six or seven shipwrights were working there. All the frames were set in place and secured to the keel, and much of the planking was complete. Two of the shipwrights were drilling and driving in and clenching the nails. The stern was there, with the transom secured and the guides for taking the rudder about to be put in place. High up on the vessel another shipwright was shaping a large piece of timber, using a long-handled, broad-bladed tool for the curve of the gunwale. 'That tool?' Robert said. 'It's called an adze.' The blade was very sharp, and able to take wafer-thin shavings off the timber, to give it its final shape. The boat when complete would be fifty feet long. 'That's a lot of fish,' Robert said.

When the tour was over, they made their way to the yard entrance, and there they were met by John, who had been waiting for a matter of only ten minutes or so. He thanked his cousin for taking so much time and trouble with his sons. 'Why yes,' they echoed. 'We've enjoyed it immensely.'

'Ah well in that case you must come to the launch. Bring the whole family.'

'Just say when,' said John.

It would happen in about two months' time.

On the way home, the lads asked their father what the launch would entail.

'Well,' said John, 'when a newly built boat is first put to sea, it's given a name.'

'How do they get it into the sea?'

'Usually on greased timbers, sliding down the slipway.'

Launch of the new fishing boat

AFTER JUST under two months or so Robert called again. It was one evening, and he'd come to give them a date for the launch. 'The last Saturday in June,' he said. 'Two o'clock.' That was when the tide was suitable. Everyone got up early when the day came round, and once some essential work around the farm was done they got themselves dressed up and set off in the wagon. They were met by Robert and his wife Alice, who wore a flowery dress and short jacket. Robert had a dark suit with matching waistcoat, and a striped tie, and to top it had a black bowler hat. In his waistcoat he had a Hunter pocket watch on a loop of gold chains. His boots were black and laced, trimmed with grey spats. To John and his family he looked the picture of elegance, especially when he twirled his moustache.

There had been a viewing platform built, and they went there now to watch the ceremony. Already there were a number of

Robert's friends, as well as the owner of the yard and the master shipwright. Robert introduced them. One of the friends was a Methodist minister, who said a prayer for those destined to sail in the boat.

The master shipwright checked that the shores below had been cleared, then gave the signal that the vessel was ready for launch. Alice, who'd been asked to name the boat, came forward and broke a bottle of wine on the fore end of the vessel. 'I name this fishing boat *New Surprise*,' she said. The craftsmen underneath the vessel knocked away the last of the shores, and the boat slid down on its greased ways into the water. A system of wires moored it to the shore. The guests now made their way to the main building, where a buffet meal was waiting.

Someone asked Robert about the future of his new boat. 'It'll be fitted out in about a fortnight,' he said, 'then start fishing off Devon and Cornwall.'

'And where will it be based?'

'Falmouth, naturally.'

While John and Elizabeth were talking to Robert and his wife, the three Toye brothers had sneaked back to the tables and were eating huge cream buns – a fact that couldn't be disguised by the jam that streaked their cheeks. They were thinking, wrongly, that no one would take much notice. However, their father had seen them and beckoned them away from the table. They scoffed the last of their buns, and complied. John and his wife made a move to depart, excusing themselves. 'A few more jobs to do about the farm,' John said. 'Thanks for asking us, and thanks for an excellent meal.'

'You know you're always welcome.'

'You must come and see *us*,' said Elizabeth.

As they drove away they waved goodbye.

'Now that was *such* a great experience,' Sandy said. 'You know, I would love to go to sea in a fishing boat.'

'There's plenty of time for that,' his father said. For now he should concentrate on the farm.

Freddie learns about the countryside

AFTER THE blizzard and snows in March, a cold spring and summer followed. Snow still lay on the hilltops in June, and when it melted there were numerous rock- and earth-falls, though thankfully none of them blocked the roads. The snow lay in the fields for several weeks into the spring, and that made ploughing and planting late. The cold summer delayed the harvest, with the root crops and cereals very much retarded by the standards of previous years. It meant that other than his dairy work and milk deliveries, Sandy had more spare time in the evenings than he'd normally expect. As his mother was recovering from an illness, he gave her time to rest – even at weekends – by taking Freddie, who'd become over-active, for walks around the farm and into the countryside. He took him along the roads, where he showed him the different types of birds darting in and out of the hedgerows.

During one walk Sandy pointed out a very small bird with a streaky brown plumage, and a grey head and breast. Just as Sandy told him what the bird was (a Dunnock), identified by its warbling, it issued a loud lone piping note. 'Why's it do that then?' Freddie asked.

'To draw attention to other Dunnocks.'

On another walk Freddie was shown the kind of places where mistle thrushes lived. 'Listen. You can hear one,' Sandy said. There was a clear whistle from on high in a treetop. Then for a change one day Sandy took him in the wagon when he was delivering milk. When all his calls had been made, he drove the wagon up to the woods above the farm. They tethered the horse and took a stroll, delighting in all the brown squirrels scampering up the trees with the nuts they had found on the ground. Farther into the woods they reached a clearing. 'Now, just you be quiet,' Sandy said. Ahead of them were three crows, one of which was young, all ruffling their black plumage in a sunny flash of green. They were hopping along and stopped at a dead rabbit, which they picked at. When they had eaten their fill they flew up into the trees, with a kraa-kraa noise. 'Look,' said Sandy, 'there's the nest.'

'Where? I can't see.'

'High up in that fork. Can't you see? It's made of twigs and sticks.'

On their way back to the wagon, walking down the hill, two large hares behind them bounded over the grass. They watched them for some time, cavorting, before they drove home. At a remote cottage under the hill Sandy caught sight of an old woman dressed in black, with a black cat motionless beside her. They seemed to be staring right at them. Sandy stiffened in his seat.

'What's wrong?' Freddie asked. At first Sandy didn't explain, but once they were well away from the cottage he relaxed.

'It's just a superstition,' he said.

'What's a superstition?'

'It's when you think one thing's going to make another thing happen, or when you believe in folklore.'

'What's folklore?'

'It's when someone like that old lady everyone thinks is a witch.'

On another outing Sandy took his brother to the hollow where he'd discovered the Celtic remains. He showed him exactly how he'd made the discovery, and enthused that even after all this time you could still see the outline of the burial site, despite the intervening rock-falls. Freddie, ever curious, climbed much farther up the hill, and just as he was about to turn he saw a cave that the more recent falls had uncovered. It was still partly obscured by gorse bushes. Sandy raced up to the spot. Both of them went inside, then stopped suddenly when a flutter of wings brushed their faces. Freddie was reluctant to go any further.

'It's all right,' Sandy said. 'They're only birds.' He went ahead of him, climbing up the slope of what seemed to him a man-made tunnel, cut into the soft rock at the back of the cave. After a few yards he could see daylight. Freddie, still a little timid, followed him. They eventually came out in a large upper cave with a flat area beyond it projecting out from the rock-face high up on the hill. When they looked out they could see for miles into the countryside, all the way down to the River Helford. After admiring the view, they looked around inside the cave. It had been inhabited at one time or other, as there were lots of small animal bones strewn about. There were charred patches here and there, which indicated fires and habitation. There were also carvings on the walls, which bore a remarkable similarity to those from the hollow. On retracing their steps and coming out into the open they looked up towards the main cave above, and now realised why they couldn't see it from below. The platform at the front of the cave, with its rock-face projection, hid it perfectly.

Freddie was quite excited with what they'd discovered. Sandy warned him they would have to tell their father, who was sure to be angry (particularly with him, Sandy), for what they had done had quite possibly been very dangerous. He did however expect their father to come out himself and take a look, and might even invite the archaeologist back. Sure enough, when they got home, covered in dust, it was blindingly clear they'd been doing quite a bit more than delivering milk. When the truth was out, their father was furious – just as Sandy predicted. 'You of all people ought to know better,' he shouted. 'What if there'd been another rock-fall, eh?'

'Don't know, Father.'

'It doesn't bear thinking about!'

'Sorry, Father.'

'Mm, well – it does sound interesting nevertheless. Perhaps you'll take me up there and show me the cave.'

During the following week he did in fact go up there, and curious about the carvings contacted Mr Jago, the archaeologist in Truro, who paid a visit some weeks later.

By September the root crops and cereals were ready to harvest, and that was work Sandy had to help with. Because they were late they had to be lifted quickly and taken to market before the weather changed. Everyone worked hard – Joe, Sandy, their father, the farm hands – for the next two weeks. When the work was done, Sandy sometimes took Freddie to the harbour at Falmouth to sail his yacht.

Autumn activities

THE NEXT month was colder with intermittent showers. Sandy had to help on what dry days there were with the rest of the root crops. These would be kept for his mother to use in the winter months, as well as for feeding the animals. Towards the end of the month Sandy had to take on more of the digging, as Joe had badly bruised a leg in a fall while repairing a barn roof, and was now able to carry out only general maintenance around the farm. Thereafter there was little else to do. However, as the Richards' farm was on much higher ground, the harvesting there was even later. To make the most of a dry spell at the end of the month Richards hired his neighbour's hands to help with his crops.

This year the Halloween party was held in the Toyes' farmhouse. As Tom and Jim at that time were busy with their new jobs, and Margery felt she was too old for Halloween parties, it was left to Sandy to carry on the tradition. So that the whole thing shouldn't fall flat, Sandy's mother urged Freddie to invite some of *his* friends, from the village. She and Sandy prepared the food and organised the games. On the night itself Freddie was his usual lively self, first to duck into the tub of water and sink his teeth into an apple, and generally charging round at all the other entertainments. All the guests enjoyed it immensely, and beamed with delight and said their many thank-yous when it was over and time to leave. Most of Freddie's friends had never been to a Halloween party before.

The next event Sandy really looked forward to was the Bonallack firework party on Guy Fawkes' night. Jim had managed to leave the boat yard early, and he met Sandy at the Richards' place. Tom was away, serving his apprenticeship, but Margery was keen to go. A sizeable crowd was there when they arrived, all huddled round the bonfire as the evening was very cold. The three friends had joined it for only a matter of minutes when George Minhinick and his friends came over and started to chat. At this point Sandy noticed someone he recognised – a man called Jan Searle, who had worked as a casual labourer on the farm some two years ago. He was heavily built, of medium height, with long arms and a bull neck. His head was large and his face was puffy and florid, sign of a heavy drinker. He wore his hair long down the back of his neck. Sandy saw him pick up a log from a woodpile, then, shouting, run down a slope. On reaching one of the small displays, he smashed it with a single swing of the log, scattering its fireworks everywhere. Next he turned his attention to one of the larger displays, but this time George, Sandy and Jim ran across to restrain him. George was slightly ahead of the other two and immediately blocked Searle's advance. Searle struck at him with the log, gashing George's hand as he parried the blow. George grabbed him round the waist, but because of Searle's size couldn't bring him to ground. Presently Sandy and Jim caught up, and between them the three grappled him down.

Jim and George held his arms, while Sandy pinned his legs to the ground. Margery shouted for help to some of the ground staff on hand, who rushed over and tied Searle's hands. They led him away to the house. They said they would lock him in one of the spare rooms until he'd sobered up. They explained that Searle had been employed by the gardener here, but had been dismissed for absence and drunkenness. This was how he'd tried to get his own back.

George and the others returned to the warm shelter of the bonfire. Margery noticed that the wound to his hand was seeping blood, and so instantly took off her scarf and bound it tightly. 'You should get that seen to,' she said. He began to realise how bad the cut was, and so asked one of his friends to drive him home, where he could have it properly cleaned and dressed. Those who remained enjoyed the rest of the display, and although Jim and Sandy still felt the effects of the tussle, the consensus was it was better than the previous year's. The Bonallacks' displays just got better and better.

When it came time to start clearing up, the three friends lingered only a little longer, then made their way home. On the way, naturally the main topic of conversation was the incident with Searle, which carried on into their respective families when all had returned to the hearth.

Over the next week, Sandy heard that when Jan had sobered up he'd apologised to Mr Bonallack, having been brought before him. Bonallack was lenient, as Searle had done nothing remotely like it ever before. He told him he had to leave the district, and if he ever made trouble round here again, his night's doings would be reported to the Falmouth Borough Police.

Preparation for winter and Mrs Richards' birthday party

WINTER CAME early in southern Cornwall in 1891, the conditions cold and drizzly. Sandy felt the dampness in his bones. It was not a season he enjoyed. As usual, it was the time when his mother did most of her bottling and preserves, which he would help her with once he'd finished his dairy work. He liked the kitchen smells – the onions, herbs and vinegar – and always had reminders of the pleasures of Christmas.

In the kitchen one day, he found her with a freestanding oven with a large copper pan full of milk on the top, being heated. The fuel was charcoal inside the oven on a grill, which although a slow process was ideal for raising the cream. Sandy asked where she'd got the oven from, and she said an old aunt she'd visited near Constantine had given it her.

When he'd finished work, Sandy went up to the Richards' farm, as he wanted to find out when Tom was next coming home. Mrs Richards was playing the piano when he got there, and seemed to have recovered from her injuries well, though she still had a slight limp. Tom was coming home on the following Friday, he learned. When Sandy left, it was Margery who saw him to the door. 'The reason he's coming *next* Friday,' she said, 'is it's our mother's fortieth birthday.' She had had a letter from him a few days ago, asking her to arrange a get-together between the four friends for the Saturday afternoon – the day after the birthday party. Sandy said he'd make sure he was free. 'Good,' she said. 'I'll get a note to Jim.'

'Wonderful! I'll see you then.' He went home whistling.

Sandy's mother and father went to the party, dressed to the nines, leaving Sandy and Joe to baby-sit the ever-active Freddie. Sandy didn't mind very much, as he was tired after some barn repairs, and couldn't have managed much more than the few games of ludo he played with his brother.

Tom Richards' weekend return

ON THE Saturday after the party Sandy strolled up to the Richards' place, where Jim's pony and cart were already parked. When Sandy knocked at the door, it was Tom himself who answered and ushered him in. Margery and Jim were sitting talking near the range in the kitchen, so now they all sat round at the large deal table. 'Well,' said Sandy, 'how do you like living in Redruth? And working in a mine?' Tom was very enthusiastic in his reply. The aunt and uncle he was staying with treated him like a second son (their own son, John, being several years older than Tom). His aunt was on his mother's side, and had the family's same easy-going outlook. Tom's uncle worked where he did, at the Gwennap mine, and so they travelled together every day. In his first week there he had introduced him to all the craftsmen.

The engineer Tom was apprenticed to was called Bill Bray, a jolly man in his early forties. Whenever there was maintenance to do, or repairs to the mine's machinery, he would take Tom with him. On the first day Bill showed him the layout of the thirty-four-inch engine and the 120 stamp-heads it operated. The stamp-heads crushed the ore before it went for smelting, and were always in need of repair, Bill said. Sometimes stamp axles needed to be replaced, and if so, quickly. The most important thing was to ensure that the pumps were always well maintained, as it was these that took water off the lower levels of the mine. Tom was allowed to undertake some simple repairs to them, under Bill's guidance. 'In some of the older mines,' he said, 'workmen are known to have drowned, due to rock-falls, and the flooding that caused.' The older pumps couldn't cope with the sheer volume and velocity of water.

Other than his apprenticeship, Tom attended the Camborne School of Mines several evenings each week. The school's principal was a J J Beringer. In his first year he'd be taking basic subjects. The ones he liked were elementary analysis, magnetism and electricity. It was a four-year course, and if he passed his exams the award was an engineering certificate.

Jim turned attention to Tom's sister. 'What have you been up to,' he said, 'since the firework display?'

'Mostly running the farmhouse,' she replied.

'Oh yes, of course, your mother's accident. How is she?'

'She's better.'

'So what else have you been doing?'

She said how much she'd enjoyed studying her books on husbandry. The knowledge she had gleaned had stood her in good stead when helping her father diagnose the various minor ailments that afflicted their animals. 'But what about you, Jim?' she asked.

He'd been busy at the boat-yard, with his own apprenticeship. He said he had an excellent craftsman as his instructor, who had been chosen by his father. His name was Jim Harvey, aged about fifty, small in stature, and nearly bald (there was one stray wisp stroked lovingly from temple to temple). Jim had shown him how to make his own tools – wooden planes, mallets, scribes. More recently he'd shown him how to select the timber you'd use according to the repair you had to make. When, after so many years, his apprenticeship came to an end, he would move to the drawing office, and there receive further training.

Finally it was Sandy's turn. He said that most of his time since leaving school had been spent looking after the dairy, and that had been ever more the case when his mother wasn't well. He'd had a week's trip on a fishing boat, arranged by Mr Minhinick — to catch pilchards off the Cornish coast. That, quite apart from having seen the building and launch of his second cousin's fishing boat, had made him all the more eager to go to sea. 'I do doubt though,' he said, 'whether my father will release me from the farm. It makes me sad.'

At that point Mrs Richards came into the kitchen, and cheered him up with the supper she prepared. When it was time to go, Tom said that if anyone was interested he may be able to get his uncle to show them round the mine, and possibly the mining school also.

Preparations for Christmas and an unusual happening

IN THE weeks closing December the Toye family were mainly preoccupied with Christmas. As there was little work to do around the farms Sandy's mother and Mrs Richards volunteered to help at the church hall making the nativity scene — the infant Jesus with the three kings in attendance. The latter were made by a local artist. The two farm ladies made up the drapes and provided the straw to line the enclosure, with the enclosure itself built by Sandy's father. Some of the helpers painted it. When the work was done it all looked very life-like.

On the approach to Christmas, Sandy's father asked him to help with choosing presents for Freddie and Joe (he'd already got a fob watch for Sandy's mother) on a trip to Falmouth. They began their expedition in the bookshop and general store. Sandy chose some books for his mother, Freddie and Joe, while his father picked out some puzzles and games. Before they returned home, John had some business in town, so Sandy said he'd meet him later at the harbour. At the harbour, although there were several fishing boats in, he couldn't see the one with the sailor he'd befriended. His father wasn't long in coming, and when he did so had bought them lunch (which they ate in the wagon, looking out to sea).

Back at the farm, Sandy crept in stealthily and hid the presents. Christmas Day itself passed off much as usual, with a light breakfast followed some hours later by a sumptuous feast. Afterwards they retired to the parlour to open their presents. Sandy's mother was overjoyed with the fob watch, and with the books from the boys. Sandy and Joe also received books, and pocket knives too, while Freddie had books of his own and puzzles. John had a silver-topped cane from his wife. When Sandy weighed his new knife from hand to hand, he was glad his father couldn't read his mind, for he imagined all sorts of uses for it in something other than farming.

In the evening Freddie was put to bed after playing with his new games, and the rest settled down to their reading. Presently there were several loud knocks at the door, and when John went to answer, there on the doorstep was a man he recognised as Joe Beal, a hand he had previously hired. He was swaying a lot, but trying to hold his balance. He stank of beer and was obviously drunk. John caught him as he fell.

They helped him indoors to the kitchen, where they made him strong black coffee. Joe recovered slightly, if still slurring when he spoke, though when he quaffed more of the coffee did muster an apology, and suddenly seemed embarrassed. He said, coyly, he'd been invited for a drink with friends who lived near the farm. Being a widower with no family he took up the offer, as he was, to be honest, a very lonely man – especially so at this time of year. He'd been ill recently and was still on medication, but even so he didn't think a few drinks would do him any harm. On his way home, however, he began to feel dizzy. It got worse and he started to hallucinate. Then he lost his way and took a wrong turn, but had somehow found himself here at the Toyes'.

Everyone was reasonably sympathetic. After another mug of coffee, and a slice of cake, he felt much better. As he didn't seem to want to budge, John hitched up the wagon and insisted it was no trouble at all taking him home.

Illness hits the Toye family

WITH NO let-up in the weather through January, everyone felt depressed, though worse was to come. The weekend before Freddie was due back in school he was taken ill. He developed a chesty cough with a high temperature, and was flushed and perspiring — even with little exertion. His mother put him to bed with a stoneware hot water bottle, and lit a fire in his grate. Next day he was feverish, and it seemed likely the doctor would have to be called. It so happened that Mrs Richards dropped by to see them, and on hearing about Freddie asked if she could look in on him. When she did so she said his symptoms were much like Tom's when he had had a chesty cold. Best remedy was a hot bread and mustard poultice wrapped in muslin and placed on the chest. They tried it. It certainly made Freddie sweat, and it wasn't too uncomfortable either. Later, he seemed a little better.

When John came in from his morning's work he heard what had happened. He went upstairs and found Freddie somewhat more cheerful and certainly breathing easier. He expressed himself wholly impressed with Mrs Richards' remedy, and while on business in Falmouth the following day said he would call in at Freddie's school and report the illness. When he talked to

Freddie's teacher, the latter was surprised at the news, as Freddie always seemed so well and full of energy. He did though have a twinkle in his eye and a smile on his face when he said that on his return, perhaps Freddie would be a little less boisterous, for a couple of days anyway. John smiled too. However, on returning home he found that another member of his family had been taken ill. This time it was Joe, with the same coughing and the same high temperature. His eyes were swollen and his face was a shade of beetroot. Like Freddie, he had been sent to bed, and had a hot water bottle and a fire. For the time being, Sandy had to take over his work, as well as attend to his own with the dairy.

In the afternoon, Sandy's father said *he* wasn't feeling well. In the evening he had a bout of coughing, and so went to bed early and tried to shake it off. Next day he was feeling worse, and added to the coughing was a high temperature. He was forced to stay in bed. Sandy was called up to his room and told what jobs had to be done. 'You'll need to see Jim Pollard too,' he said, 'about the vegetables for market.'

The following day Sandy was struck down too, so *he* took to his bed. That left his mother running up and down stairs, what with sandwiches, water bottles, drinks and everything else. 'I don't know! This place is worse than a cottage hospital!' she said. Luckily, she kept going, and didn't become ill herself.

By the end of the week John and his two eldest boys had recovered, and Freddie was up and about for a few hours each day. By the following Monday everyone was back to normal, though Freddie was taken to school, rather than walk. As one might imagine, there was plenty of catching up to do around the farm. They were hoping that February would bring them better luck.

A sailing ship stranded on the rocks

FOR THE next two weeks the weather was reasonably dry and calm, but this soon changed, the lull followed by high winds that blew down tress and damaged buildings, though the neighbouring farms suffered only a few loose slates. Sandy heard from one of the hands that a sailing ship had been cast on to the rocks near Falmouth, and was quite severely damaged. As Tom was home for the weekend, he went up to the Richards' place and told him and his sister about it. The three of them took a trip down to the coast to see where the ship was stranded. They were able to survey it from the cliff-top high above the wreckage, then went down to where a small group of people had gathered round the rocks. The ship was wedged fast between the huge boulders, while the sea slammed and foamed its hull and splintered its planking. Some of the timbers had broken free and were bobbing on the waves. There were barrels, items of clothing and many of the ship's fittings littering the rocks, or simply pushed inland under the force of the waves. The main mast was broken, with its canvas torn, twisted and tattered.

Sandy looked about for anyone he could recognise. Just apart from the crowd was the old man they had met in the cave at Falmouth, shaking his head and looking quite distressed. Tom asked someone where the crew were now. They were safe, someone said, with only minor injuries. They were with the coastguard.

They were just going to leave when the three friends heard someone in the crowd say there was a dog barking in the ship. Some of the young men decided to rescue it. They fetched a long rope from a house nearby and climbed down nearer the ship. One of them tied it round his waist while the others held it firmly at the other end. Then he waded out. He scrambled up and over the gunwale, and remained motionless for a moment listening out for the dog. He could hear it barking in a cabin just below the deck. He untied himself, then climbed down into the cabin, where he soon located and scooped the dog up. He re-attached the rope, and with the dog in his arms eased himself back over the gunwale and waded into the water. It was difficult, holding the dog, and he slipped several times. The others tugging at the rope had their work cut out. However, after a determined effort the young man reached the flats below the cliff, whereupon everyone cheered. A woman who recognised the dog took charge of it.

The three friends had much to tell their folk when they got back home that evening. 'Don't have nightmares,' his mother said, when Sandy climbed the stairs to bed.

Jim Pollard and his family trapped in their storm-damaged cottage

WORK AROUND the farm went up several fold in the month that followed. The fields had to be de-stoned again, and the drains were ready for their annual repair. This year the bulk of the ploughing was carried out by Sandy's brother Joe, as Jim had hurt his back. He'd twisted himself lifting heavy loads from the wagon. He tried to persuade Joe to enter the ploughing competition, but despite his undoubted competence Joe didn't feel at all confident.

The weather in March was much better than in the previous year, so ploughing for John's rotation of crops was over in good time. This allowed an early planting and good selection of crops. The weather remained calm, but at the end of the month it deteriorated rapidly. Strong winds all over southern Cornwall rapidly assumed storm conditions, and that did damage to many a house in and around Falmouth – with one unusual incident affecting the Pollard cottage. It was towards the end of March. The Toye family had retired to bed early after an exhausting day of work. The wind had hampered their planting. John suddenly woke late in the night, having heard an urgent knock at the door. Groggy and half-awake he climbed out of bed. He put on his trousers hastily over his flannelette nightshirt. Then he went downstairs. 'Who's there?' he shouted.

'George. George Pollard. Jim's son. Open up, please.'

He opened the door and bundled the boy inside, out of the howling wind. George was breathless, having run all the way from home, which was about half a mile from the farm – a real struggle against the force of the wind. He told John that a large tree overhanging the cottage had been uprooted and crashed down on the roof of their cottage. His father and mother were trapped in the back room, pinned down by the roof beams. George had escaped only because he slept in the front room.

John told the boy to stay in the hall while he got his two sons, Joe and Sandy. While they were getting dressed he went back to his room and told his wife. When he came out, Joe and Sandy were ready. They fetched crowbars and sturdy poles from the barn, and having harnessed the horse to the wagon were off. On reaching the cottage they tethered the horse at a safe distance, then grabbed their tools. They cleared the stones and debris blocking the heavy beams that pinned the couple down, then set to with their crowbars shifting what masonry had jammed in the beams themselves. After that they were able to bring in two heavy poles, which they inserted under the piece of timber bearing down on Jim. Putting pressure on it, they managed to lift it clear of his body. Then they wedged a stone under the beam to stop it slipping back. Gradually, Jim was eased out, in a very painful state. They took him outside and very gently lifted him on to the wagon. Next they set about getting Alice out, who although trapped had managed to crawl under the bed. They used a heavy pole as before, and having got the beam off the bed secured it by wedging another stone. Then they lifted her clear of the wreckage, and soon had her reunited with her husband, outside groaning in the wagon.

'Right,' said John, 'Let's get them back to the farmhouse.'

'What about the crowbars?' Sandy said.

'Leave 'em. We'll come back later.'

They set off for the farmhouse at a slow and gentle pace, not wanting to aggravate the pain in Jim's back. When they got there they lifted him and Alice very carefully off the wagon and took them inside. Elizabeth met them in the hall and suggested taking the two casualties into the spare room downstairs.

'A good idea,' said John. 'Jim'll never climb the stairs in his state.'

They took them and laid them on the floor, then fetched some spare mattress from upstairs and bedding from the storeroom. When they'd got the two settled, it looked as if Alice had only a bruised shoulder and cuts to her face. Jim, however, was still in agony with his back, apart from other wounds. Elizabeth brought in a basin of hot water and washed away the blood, and treated their cuts with iodine. John meanwhile sent Joe and Sandy out in the wagon to call the doctor. 'You can pick up the poles and crowbars,' he said, 'on the way back.'

Elizabeth looked after George. Then, after about half an hour, Joe and Sandy returned, and having stabled the horse and stowed everything away in the barn came inside for a good hot drink. Their mother had made up a bed in Sandy's room for George, and the three boys – tired after all this excitement – went off and tried to get some sleep. Soon the doctor arrived. He examined Jim thoroughly, and found him only badly bruised, with no bones broken, and, crucially, no damage to his spinal column. He told him he would have to rest for quite some time as the bruising was very severe. He looked at Alice next, who had suffered only light bruising to the shoulder. She had been lucky, he said. He left, with instructions for John and Elizabeth as to treatment.

Later in the day, after Jim and Alice had, thankfully, slept, Elizabeth made them a meal. Joe and Sandy, bleary-eyed after their interrupted sleep, plodded off outside and finished the work they had started the previous day. They toiled hard until midday, then returned for something to eat. George was called down, having slept on. In the afternoon John went in to see the boy's parents, to ask how they were. Alice was feeling better, but Jim was still in pain, though that had eased somewhat with the medication the doctor had given him. John quizzed him about the accident. His senior hand explained that the tree overhanging the cottage had been uprooted by the wind's unrelenting ferocity, and had crashed through the roof – an eventuality, he said, that could have been avoided. The tree had been partially uprooted in a previous storm, so the warning signs were there, and he'd meant to cut it down. 'Always just too busy,' he said.

Later in the day Elizabeth and Alice took the wagon and drove over to the cottage to collect some clothes and other things. For the next few days Alice busied herself in the kitchen with Elizabeth, while her husband remained confined to bed – strictly doctor's orders. By the end of the week he had recovered to the point of shuffling round the house without too much pain. With that in mind, on the Saturday morning John had something to show them. 'Put on your coats,' he said. He drove them right to the other side of the farm, pulling up at a cottage gate. He produced a key and led them up the path. 'Go on, open up,' he said. 'It's yours.' He'd bought the cottage last year after the person living there had died. He'd planned to give it to his son as a gift when he married, but clearly that wasn't going to be just yet.

While they were looking round he said it was theirs rent-free until their own cottage had been repaired. They were overjoyed at his generosity.

'Nonsense,' said John. 'You deserve it. Good people are so hard to find.'

The friends crew a fishing boat from Porth Navas to Durgan

FOR THE next fortnight or so Sandy and Joe were ever busy on the farm, what with Jim still out of commission largely, able to perform light duties only. That apart, they helped their father move furniture and fittings into the new cottage, and it wasn't many days before Alice and Jim were ready to move in and make it home. The Toye family came over to the house-warming, and were praised in a speech from Jim over the meal, in which he gave thanks once again for John and Elizabeth's kindness and hospitality. Not long after that, Jim was back at work and carrying on with his normal duties at the farm. This eased the workload for Sandy and Joe. Sandy was especially pleased, as he hadn't visited the Richards family for several weeks, and so didn't know when Tom was next due home. He went up there one evening, and was met by Margery who took him to the parlour. Her mother and father were reading. They looked up and asked him what had kept him away so long. Sandy told them all about the cottage, and how the Pollards had had to be re-housed, and the injury to Jim. 'It's meant I've really been kept busy,' he said.

'You poor lad,' Mrs Richards said.

'Oh, I'm used to it.'

'I expect you want to know when Tom's coming home.'

'As a matter of fact, that's why I called.'

Margery said it wouldn't be until the end of April. This was partly to suit plans Jim Earle had made.

'What are they then?' Sandy asked.

'Jim did call on you to tell you actually, but no one was around.' Jim's father was completing a repair on a small fishing boat on his slip at Porth Navas. Work was scheduled for completion by the end of April. He wanted hands to crew the boat so that it could be sailed, or, if there was insufficient wind, towed with a rowing boat, down the creek and along the river to Durgan. There the vessel's owner would check it over and, if satisfied, pay for the repair. The crew would then row back to Porth Navas, and there the four friends could stay at the bunkhouse over the weekend.

Sandy was keen. 'Just love that bunkhouse,' he said. He thought his father would allow him time off, so Margery said she'd write to Tom as well as Jim and let them know. When Sandy told his father, John agreed that he deserved a weekend off. Until then, he continued to work hard.

On his birthday, the 21st of April, Sandy was given another day off. As it was a dry day, he walked to Falmouth, where he visited a tailor's. After much indecision he bought a pair of trousers, which he left behind for later collection. After looking round some other shops, he stepped into a teashop, and there bought himself a hot cup and a slice of cake. It was the first time he had eaten out on his own. Next he strolled to the harbour for a look along the wall at the fishing boats and other vessels berthed. One he picked out was a fishing boat owned by Mr

Minhinick, whose captain was out on deck stowing some nets. Sandy asked if he needed an extra seaman. 'Sorry, no,' came the reply. 'I've got a full crew as it is.' Sandy thanked him and carried on to the end of the harbour wall, where he looked out to sea and dreamed of all the voyages he felt he was destined to make. All too soon he blinked himself back to reality, and remembering his trousers made his way back to the tailor's, and having collected them went back home.

His birthday meal was a relaxed and happy affair. After it the family retired to the parlour, where Sandy was given his presents. From his father he got a colourful waistcoat, which his mother insisted he had to try on. 'My my,' she said, 'it makes you quite grown up.' Between them she and Joe gave him a belt with a silver buckle. Freddie's gift was a model fishing boat, which Joe had helped him make in the workshop. Little did the family know what visions it conjured in Sandy's mind. 'Thank you all so much,' he said. 'What an end to a perfect day!'

The days to the end of the month seemed to flash by, what with so much work to do on the farm, so the weekend of their trip arrived in next to no time. Come the Friday, after his milk deliveries, he ambled up to the Richards' farm, his haversack stuffed with food and a change of clothes. When he got there Tom and Margery were loading up their wagon, and once he'd added his things they were off.

Jim was waiting when they reached the slip, and had already opened the bunkhouse. First thing they did was sit around at the kitchen table, catching up on each other's news. When they'd finished drinking tea Jim started to cook his perennial fish, while the others spread out what they had brought. After the meal Jim gave them a more detailed account of what was required of them on the trip to Durgan. Thereafter they had an early night, and in the morning one of the shipwrights came and stoked the boiler, that being required to operate the winch that hauled the vessel down the slip. An hour later Jim's father arrived and woke them up. He told them he and the shipwright would prepare the boat, and that they would be called on to man it before it was afloat. By the time they'd removed the shores it was high tide and the water was rising.

When the four friends had finished breakfast they locked up the bunkhouse and walked to the slip, where they climbed on board the boat. Jim's father was already on board himself, and started to give them their final instructions. The shipwright cleared more of the shores, then connected the winch and gradually tightened the wire until taut enough to haul the boat clear of the cradle. Jim knocked out the last of the shores, and that allowed the boat to be hauled completely clear. Jim's father now guided it shore-side, with the rowing boat alongside, which he roped to a bollard at the fore end. The shipwright slackened the wire, so that now Jim released it from the boat. Then he and his father climbed into the rowing boat and started to tow the fishing boat downstream. Sandy, Tom and Margery took turns on the tiller, guiding the boat out to mid-stream.

Towing continued until the boat was away from the narrow part of the creek, at which point Tom was asked to release the towrope. The rowing boat was then secured to the stern, with the rope much shortened. Here Jim and his father climbed out and on to the fishing boat. The sail was raised, and with a strong breeze behind them they made good headway. At the end of the creek they used the sail with the light wind to tack around the Pedn Billy point.

Once they were well out into the Helford, Jim's father pointed out Frenchman's Creek ahead. 'How did it get its name?' Margery asked.

'Possibly from French man-o'-wars that used the creek in the eighteenth and early nineteenth centuries.' The creek was ideal for harbouring ships under the overhanging trees.

The wind was stronger on the river, and they were soon at Helford Passage. They had to adjust the sails and tack around the headland, passing Polgwidden Cove before turning to the north bank to Durgan. Once there they dropped anchor, and all of them climbed into the rowing boat, with Sandy and Tom rowing them to shore. After tying up, Jim's father called on the boat-owner, and the four friends strolled to the jetty. There the three lads decided to go for a swim, and after changing into their swimsuits made for the beach. Margery sat it out at the jetty, and watched. The lads waded slowly through what turned out to be very cold river water, slipping on the seaweed. All three of them ended up falling in, at which Margery roared with laughter. After a short swim they returned to shore and dried off quickly.

When they had dressed themselves they went for a walk with Margery into the village, which had a school and a field with donkeys. 'Surprising to see those,' Margery said, 'in a fishing village.' Jim said that as there were no roads out of Durgan, donkeys were a principal means of transportation. It was also the case that fish brought into port was loaded into panniers, strapped to the donkeys, and taken to the market at Falmouth. After a brief look round they returned to the jetty and had their lunch.

Meanwhile Jim's father was out at the boat with its owner, who said that the finish was good and the standard high. The two men returned to his cottage, where the bill was settled.

The row back to Porth Navas took them quite some time. The river was tidal, and the tide was not in their favour. All except Margery took it in turns to row, but as the wind eased off that task became easier. Now at last Margery did take a turn, in her brother's place, and was paired with Sandy for the last leg back to the slip. It was now early evening. Jim's father thanked the four friends, but before leaving them said there were some large Cornish pasties waiting for them, which his wife had prepared.

After their feast, they all felt suddenly tired, and were soon tucked up asleep in bed.

The Pollard family return to their old cottage after repairs

WORK ON the farm for Sandy at this time of year was hoeing weeds in the vegetable fields, and the dairy as usual. There was another task, however, and that was rebuilding the Pollards' cottage, which he helped Joe and his father to do. The beams were measured up and new ones ordered, and replacement joists came from the joiner's shop in Falmouth. Before work could commence, all the debris had to be cleared, and it was necessary also to hire a stonemason, to re-dress the stone and make good the damaged walls (for only then could the beams be fitted). With those in place, and the joists cut, John told his two sons that he'd run out of nails, and had to go back for more. 'Take a break,' he said. Thinking his father would be away for some time, Sandy climbed on to one of the roof beams and demonstrated a balancing act, edging along with a heavy pole to stabilise his weight. Joe simply laughed. However, John returned earlier than expected, and although amused himself had to do the fatherly thing and show that he was furious. 'Get down at once – and don't you dare do that again,' he shouted. Both boys were embarrassed to have been caught not working – especially Sandy, who returned to his jobs red-faced.

With the nails hammered into the joists, the roof slates now had to be fitted and secured. While this was going on, Jim was repairing the windows and door, and Alice made new curtains.

Later, the window frames and other woodwork took a lick of paint, and soon the whole thing looked like new. When it was time to move back in, Sandy and Joe helped them with the furniture – three wagon-loads in fact. During this process, Sandy noticed two items that sparked his curiosity. The first looked like an old lamp – a type he had never seen before – and the second was an empty jar that smelt of fish. 'Oh, the lamp,' said Alice. 'That's an old stonen chill.' By that she meant an earthenware lamp. Its well had several lips moulded on its rim, and it held about a pint of 'train oil' (or pilchard oil), with a wick made from the pithy core of a rush. The 'train oil', which was purchased locally, was produced when the catch of pilchards was placed in hogsheads back at port. With holes in the barrel, and pressing down with heavy weights, all the oil oozed out. 'That other thing,' she said, 'is a bussa.' That was a jar used to store pilchards pickled in brine as one of many winter supplements.

When the work was done, Alice gave everyone a cold drink. On returning home, Sandy and Joe found the others in the parlour, where Sandy said the Pollards had more or less settled back in, but was much more interested to tell them about the stonen chill and bussa. 'Oh yes,' said his mother, 'they're still in common use in many of the fishermans' cottages.' Grown-ups were very wise.

The Land's End to John O'Groats cycle race

ONE EVENING, after finishing work, when Sandy went up to the Richards' place, Margery led him to the kitchen, as her parents had guests in the parlour. 'You been in touch with Tom or Jim?' he asked. Margery said her parents had had a letter from Tom, which didn't tell of plans for an imminent visit home. 'And I haven't seen Jim,' she added. She did go on to say that she intended writing to both of them, with a plan to visit Penzance, on Whit Monday, the 5th of June – to see a man called T A Edge. Edge was a famous cyclist, attempting a cycle record, from Land's End to John O'Groats. It had been well publicised in the local press, so a good turnout was expected, lining a part of the route near Penzance. Afterwards they could spend the day there.

'Count me in,' said Sandy.

By the following week, Margery had had replies from the other two, who were also interested. Tom would be home for a long weekend, and Jim would make sure that Monday was free, and would drive over. All went according to plan, and so on the 5th of June the four friends were off on the road to Penzance. When they got to the spectator site, a good many were already there, some with cycles of their own. They found themselves a good spot, and there waited for the pacemakers, then the man himself to whiz by. After about half an hour, the cyclist approached, and was coming at a good speed. An enthusiast from one of the local cycling clubs estimated his speed at fourteen mph. He was without pacemakers – who for this stage were not available – and the crowd gave him a cheer. One Mr Siddeley, of the Anfield Bicycle Club, who had organised this latest record attempt, arrived later on a bike himself, as there were no trains from Land's End. He also was given a cheer.

Once Edge and the officials were clear, the fun really started. Would-be cyclists on penny-farthings, boneshakers and any other type of ancient two-wheeler, tried to emulate the famous T A Edge. Most cycled too fast for the bikes they had, and were soon skidding on loose stones or slipping in the mud or cowpats. Some landed in ditches. With cheers and roars of laughter ringing in their ears, they slunk away, knees skinned to boot, but with no serious injuries.

When the crowd had started to disperse, the four friends decided to carry on to the beach at Penzance, which was about half a mile away. After a picnic there, they took off their boots and stockings and ran into the sea, where they paddled, amid much splashing. The three lads decided to have a skimming competition, and so rushed out and had soon selected enough flat stones for the job. Margery remained in the water, searching for colourful shells.

Tom eventually won. They all went off to collect Margery, who seemed quite contented one moment, then suddenly cried out, obviously in pain. They splashed into the water after her and getting close saw a pinky-looking liquid swirling round her feet. Sandy and Tom lifted her out and got her to the shore, where they could see that part of a razor shell was embedded in her foot, with blood seeping out. They helped her to the wagon. Tom tore up some strips of cloth in the waggon, while Sandy pulled the razor shell out. (That must have been painful, but she remained tight-lipped.) Tom wrapped the strips of cloth tight round the wound to staunch the blood, but with the loss of so much she was pale and in a state of shock. Jim covered her with a blanket, and with the three lads' jackets.

When Sandy saw how bad it was he knew that they must take her to hospital. They set off apace, Tom driving as fast as he could. Once there two porters with a trolley wheeled her to the operating theatre, the three lads following close behind, and very concerned by now at the depth of blood soaking the cloth. A doctor joined them presently, who got one of the nurses to clean the wound. That done, he administered a local anaesthetic and closed it and stitched it. The nurse then applied a proper bandage.

The doctor complimented Tom on how well he'd bandaged his sister's foot, which had certainly prevented a more severe loss of blood. He advised them to get off home right away, and to keep her warm throughout the journey. Their parents should ask their doctor to call the next day to check for any complications. Margery was settled in the wagon with her injured foot raised up on two haversacks, while she herself was swathed in the jackets and blanket. Tom took the driving seat, while the other two stayed in the back with Margery. They got home by early evening, where Mr and Mrs Richards were surprised to see them back so soon. However, when they understood what had happened, they got their daughter off the wagon and immediately upstairs to bed, with a hot earthenware bottle.

Sandy and Jim said their farewells to Tom, who would have to return to Redruth early the next morning. They left Margery's parents with the news that they would come again mid-week, when it was hoped Margery was feeling better.

That evening Sandy told his family all about his day. His mother said she would look in at the Richards' farm the next day. The following afternoon the doctor called and examined the wound. It was healing well, he said. If she wanted to get up she could, but without putting weight on the injured foot. He would return at the end of the week with a view to removing the stitches. By the Wednesday, when Sandy and Jim paid a visit, Margery was hobbling around with a stick, and looking much better. In another week she was almost back to normal, and with the stitches out could walk, though in soft shoes only. She had no doubt she would have a scar to remind her of that fateful day in Penzance.

Later that month Sandy discovered that T A Edge had beaten the previous record by over ten hours, in a time of four days and forty minutes.

Sandy goes to sea

SANDY'S FATHER made an unusual decision. It was on a visit to Mr Minhinick, to conclude some business with the rent of his

fields. Minhinick said there was something concerning Sandy he
wished to bring up. He said that one of the ships in which he
had a part-share was in need of a seaman urgently. One of the
crew had had an accident and broken his arm. The captain needed
a replacement, as the ship was set to sail in less than a week. He
knew that Sandy was keen on the sea, and asked if he could go.
Initially John was quite emphatically not in favour of releasing
his son from the farm. It would soon be the harvest and Sandy
was needed. Minhinick calmed him down, saying he should take
some time to consider the proposal. A short voyage like this might
cure him of his wanderlust.

After some deliberation, John did agree tentatively, but wanted
to discuss it with his wife before his decision was final. 'Well,'
said Minhinick, 'if you do decide to let him go, I'll have a word
with the captain. You know, make the voyage as disagreeable as
possible, to put him off forever.'

'Good in theory,' John said. 'What's the name of the ship?'

'It's called the *Mary Edey*. Dependable little tub.'

John did talk it over with his wife, though not without
expressing his personal reservations. However, Elizabeth could
see Minhinick's reasoning, and she eventually brought her
husband round. They'd let Sandy know over their evening meal.

When Sandy got the news, he was overjoyed. He thanked them
both profusely, though his brother Joe was not so pleased (he'd
have to do Sandy's work around the farm). Next morning, after
his dairy duties, Sandy went round to Minhinick's house. He
desperately hoped he hadn't changed his mind, so it was in some
trepidation that he knocked at the door. Mr Minhinick invited him
into his office. He gave Sandy details of the duties he'd be
expected to perform, and confirmed the time he would join the
vessel on the following Monday. For the rest of the week Sandy
worked hard at his farm jobs, doing his best to ensure that not
too much was left for Joe. After his milk deliveries on Saturday

he went up to the Richards' place to tell them all about his enormous slice of luck. Tom was home for the weekend, and was really pleased for his friend. Tom's parents quizzed him almost endlessly, but eventually the three youngsters retired to the barn for a quieter chat. Margery asked him what ports the ship was bound for.

'Plymouth first, to load cargo,' Sandy said, 'then on to Gibraltar, to unload.'

'Gibraltar!'

He didn't know where the ship was bound for after that, as Mr Minhinick had given him only scant information in that regard.

'Well, have a pleasant voyage, is all I can say!'

'Thanks. I will.'

'We expect many a lurid tale when you return.'

On Monday morning Sandy went with his father to Falmouth harbour, where the ship's boat took him out to Carrick Roads, the outer anchorage. His mother said her farewells at the farmhouse, as it was too upsetting to see him board. His father waved him off, and did his best not to show any feelings. Another seaman waiting for the boat climbed in after Sandy, and once they were settled the two oarsmen rowed for the *Mary Edey*. 'You're new,' said the other seaman, who pointed out to Sandy that the Blue Peter – flag with a white square on a blue background – had been hoisted. 'That's a signal she's about to sail.'

On climbing aboard, Sandy was met by the boatswain, who explained the layout of the ship. Then he introduced him to seaman Jim Webber, who would hand him his duties during the voyage. Jim took Sandy below and showed him his locker and how to sling his hammock. After that Sandy's first task was to scrub decks – a backbreaking job – which he revelled in. That finished, Jim took him to the galley where they collected their meal, which to Sandy's amusement was dished out on wooden square plates. While they ate, Jim told him that the *Mary Edey* was a barque, having three masts, with the foremast rigged square and the after-masts rigged fore and aft.

Just before the sun went down, Sandy took a stroll on the upper deck. By now the ship was out of sight of land, and the aloneness, the grandeur of so much surrounding sea, left its impression.

Next day Jim gave him quite a few more tasks to do, and after that took him aside and gave him instruction in seamanship. He showed him how to use a sextant and read a compass, and he explained how the crew rigged and furled the sails. It was more than Sandy expected, and after over an hour of this his head was crammed with information. After the next meal the boatswain told him he could expect to be on duty for middle watch, which meant leaving his hammock heavy-eyed at midnight. Once out on deck, he would have to keep lookout until four in the morning. Nevertheless, that first night was enthralling beyond belief, with its vastness of phosphorescent sea under the dome of a star-filled sky. The breeze as it ruffled his hair thrilled every fibre of his being, and brought with it a lateral sway of the ship. A luminous ribbon of sea, with little crested waves, unfurled itself in the wake of the ship.

For the next week, whenever he could spare the time, Jim continued to offer instruction. When tested, Sandy showed that he'd taken it in. He certainly hadn't forgotten how to use a sextant or read a compass, or for that matter tie up the sails and rope systems. For the captain, this was a dilemma, for although sympathetic to so bright a new recruit, he knew he had to fulfil his promise to Sandy's father. Things had to be made difficult. His solution to that was to send Sandy aloft as often as he could, to help with setting and taking in the sails, or loosening and furling the royals. Yet this also had quite the wrong effect, spurring Sandy on to greater feats. He had a good head for heights, and being nimble had no problems climbing to the mastheads. In fact it was quite invigorating. Some days sitting on the crosstrees he looked far out to sea, occasionally seeing other ships as they passed them by. One day he even saw dolphins following the ship, a glister of sunshine lighting their scales as, with inimitable grace, they broke and dived through the surface of the water.

The storm

NEXT WEEK the ship hit rougher water crossing the Bay of Biscay. For the first time Sandy was violently sick. Fortunately Jim had some medicine he kept in a green bottle, which eased his upset stomach. As they approached the north-west part of Spain, and before following the Portuguese coast, the wind and sea grew much more turbulent. The captain knew from his barometer, and the dark clouds plainly looming ahead, that a storm was imminent. To counter it, he brought up all the crew from below, and made them loosen and furl in the sails, and drop them to the deck. The main- and mizzenmast were dispatched quickly enough, but the seamen at the foremast got their rigging tangled, a problem difficult to rectify as they now faced the full brunt of the storm. All but one of them managed to jump clear as the mast started to bend in the wind. There was a loud crack as it splintered and broke in two, leaving a stump on the deck, with the rest crashing down in a sodden flap of sails. That one unlucky seaman found himself trapped underneath it. The boatswain ordered the seamen close enough to him, which included Jim and Sandy, to lift the wreckage and free their stricken colleague. After several attempts they did get him clear. At first they feared the worst, for it very much looked as if his back was broken, though fortunately the tangle of sails and rigging had cushioned the falling timber, so saving him from serious injury. His name was George Spence. When thoroughly examined later, he was found to have only bruising to his shoulders.

Before getting back down below, the crew had to tie down as many loose things on deck as possible, including the broken mast. Then they had to batten down the hatches. When most of the seamen finally did get down, the only ones left above deck were in the wheelhouse – the helmsman, the first mate, the captain. With the storm now at its height the captain decided to let his ship ride with the wind, which would take it towards the Portuguese coast, at high speed and helter-skelter. Down below Jim and Sandy sat on their lockers, listening to the howling wind. They could hear too the two remaining masts creaking, with such deafening report they couldn't help wonder if these would also break. Above them there were barrels bouncing about, and all too often the ship was lifted clear of the water, so that it crashed back down with a sudden jolt into the turmoil of the sea. Sandy thought his time was up when water started to seep in through joints in the ship's planking. Jim allayed his fears, however, saying the volume was trivial, and they could soon bale it out after the storm had passed. For about two hours it continued unabated (which to Sandy seemed a lifetime), but then when it did subside it was as quickly as it had started. 'Ah now good,' said the captain, who told the helmsman to head for the Portuguese coast.

He had debated with the first mate whether to head for one of the Portuguese ports – either Vigo or Oporto – to carry out repairs. In the end it wasn't thought that urgent, so they sailed for Gibraltar. When the crew returned to deck, there were loose timbers, bits of broken barrel, belaying pins, and rope and tackle all over the place. This and baling out the water took them quite a bit of time to deal with, though the ship's carpenter immediately set about caulking the joints with oakum – a temporary measure. Jim and Sandy went to see the injured man, Spence, who was

166

confined to his hammock. He showed them his shoulders. The flesh was black and blue with the depth of the bruising. When they asked him how he fared he said that most of the pain was bearable, though he was very stiff. 'But I'm lucky,' he said, 'not to have broken my back.'

For the rest of the voyage there were no further troubles, and under a good strong wind they drove along south, trimming close to the Portuguese coast. Eventually the captain turned east into the Straits of Gibraltar, and on the following night they were close enough to drop anchor and heave to. Jim and Sandy came up on deck to breathe the fresh air. The two of them leaned on the gunwale together, gazing out towards the Rock. It was a clear night sky, its full moon tinged with wispy purple cloud. As Sandy looked, that sloping rock-face of Gibraltar, powdered in moonlight, was almost magical, with its town and its cluster of houses perched above the sea. 'Penny for your thoughts,' said Jim, but Sandy couldn't express them. 'Oh well, better get some rest. Tomorrow's an early call.'

Repairs to the mast and ship's hull

THE FOLLOWING morning, while the crew were preparing the ship for harbour, the captain and first mate were rowed across, and made their way to the harbour office. There the harbour master allotted them a berth, where they could unload their cargo. On their return to the ship, the captain gave orders for the ship to move into harbour. Under a favourable breeze they eased into their berth without a hitch.

While the crew were unloading, Jim and Sandy were given permission by the boatswain to help the ship's carpenter repair the mast and hull. Jim had once been employed in a joiner's shop, and as Sandy too was well used to repair work, it was a good use of their skills. They moved the broken mast onto supports that had already been prepared. Then the carpenter used a ripsaw to cut off the splintered part and leave a square end. He then used other saws and an adze to cut the mast on both sides at its base, to form a tongue. Then from the stub left on the deck he cut off the splintered fragments, to form a square end. Next, with Jim and Sandy's help, he cut a parallel groove for the tongue of the mast, using saws and chisels.

With the help of other crew members a shearlegs was erected on shore, made up of three long wooden spars that they lashed together at the upper ends, from which they suspended their lifting tackle. The lower end of the spars was secured at ground-level, by tying ropes to nearby bollards. Before the mast was lowered, the tongue and groove were coated with white lead, to help with the seal. The mast was then lowered in place slowly, to allow the tongue-end to be poised just above the stump. The carpenter, Jim and Sandy then inserted it into the groove. With the mast held firmly in place, the carpenter now drilled holes through it at the midpoint of the tongue and groove, using a large brace and bit. When there were enough holes he drove in the bolts and secured them with nuts and washers.

That job done, the seamen on shore took down and dismantled the shearlegs and ropes. The mast, although shorter, was now strong enough to take its original sails. The next task was the repair to the planking joints on *Mary Edey*'s hull. The captain had permission from the harbour master to move his ship farther along the berth, where because of a sandbank the water was shallow. This would allow the ship, much higher in the water without its cargo, to be tipped over onto its port side, leaning on the harbour wall, and held by ropes. On the starboard side, wooden shores supported the hull to prevent it tipping back. The shipside repair had to be carried out in the limited time that low water allowed – high tide would re-float the ship. Sandy and another seaman went on ahead, tearing out the oakum the water had breached. Behind them the carpenter with Jim caulked in fresh oakum, while other members of the team poured hot pitch over it to give it an extra seal. The work went well.

The starboard side repair was completed just before high tide. The shores were removed and the ropes gradually slackened, as the tide rose, which allowed the ship to re-float upright. It was then turned round, and re-berthed at the next low tide, so that the same process was now carried out on the port side. All those involved in the repair were given shore leave the following day.

Sandy is shown round Gibraltar

THE NEXT morning after breakfast Jim and Sandy left the ship and saw as much of Gibraltar as anyone can in a day. The bulk of the crew stayed behind, loading a cargo of fruit and spices. First Jim took him to the shops past the Casements, where there were heavy guns in a state of readiness for war. They reached Main Street, where most of the shops were, and looked at the wares. Sandy was fascinated by so many unusual things for sale, with most of the shops run by Indians, with their carpets and colourful silks, and a lot of brass ornamentation in the shape of lizards, tigers, dragons, and what have you. Guided by the older man, who had been here before, he bought a few knick-knacks for the family. Jim meanwhile acquired a roll of silk, which he intended to smuggle in to Falmouth, so avoiding import duty.

From Main Street they went south, passing the Governor's residence, where there were two soldiers on guard at the entrance, their tunics spotless, their buttons and boots highly polished. The building they guarded was of stone and solid-looking, and was where the Governor and his family lived. After that they carried on south past a barracks, and came to Rosia Bay. Here they climbed down to a spot with a small beach. 'After the battle of Trafalgar,' said Jim, 'Nelson's body was brought ashore here.' After some time sitting on the beach, idly gazing out towards northern Africa, Jim said it was time to eat, and knowing his way round took Sandy back down Main Street to Irish Town, where there was an inn he liked. Here they had a cooked meal. When they'd washed it down with a nice cold drink, Sandy asked if it was safe to climb the rock. 'There's a path,' Jim said, and they set off. It was hard to reach the top, and where the path ended in a sheer rock-wall they stopped to admire the view. Near them was an old castle. 'Built by the Moors,' said Jim. The Moors had occupied Gibraltar and much of Southern Spain for hundreds of years.

Suddenly a group of apes jumped down on the road close to where they were, but quickly scampered away. Sandy had only ever seen sketches of apes, in some of the books he'd got, but had never seen any running in the wild. He was fascinated with their antics and gambols, and at how obviously curious they were about *them*. 'They've been here many years,' said Jim. 'They're now protected animals.'

Looking down, Sandy could see the racecourse at the northern end of the peninsula, at which point they began their descent, and made their way to the east side. 'There's the catchment,' said Jim. This was an area cleared of vegetation, which with its natural slope drained the rainwater into a cavern and underground lake. This formed Gibraltar's fresh-water supply.

They wound their way round to a group of houses, which was a village called Catalan Bay — occupied predominantly by Italians. There were two men playing mandolins, so they stopped to listen, and even tossed them some coins. It was now getting late, however, and time to return to the ship, and as they set off a cloud began to form in the east and hang atop the Rock. When they were back down on the Spanish side, it had disappeared. 'It's called the Levant.' Jim said. 'It's a cloud unique to the Rock.'

As they carried on their way, Jim pointed out the town of La Linea, which was close to the border of Spain and Gibraltar. A village on a hill beyond that was called San Roche. Sandy asked about the trees growing on the hill. 'Those?' said Jim. 'Olive trees.' From them the locals harvested their cooking oil.

Back at the ship, the crew had almost completed loading the cargo, and under the strain of it, and the heat and humidity, the crew were sweating profusely. Jim and his young companion managed to get a meal in the galley before hiding away their purchases safe from prying eyes. Next day, before the ship sailed, a group of soldiers and their officers boarded, bound for Plymouth after their tour of duty.

The return voyage to Plymouth and Falmouth

THE SAIL to Plymouth was largely uneventful, though some crew grumbled at the overcrowding that the additional personnel had brought. Moreover the soldiers sang bawdy songs late into the night, the cause of much ill temper, especially among crew coming off watch and wanting to sleep. For his part, Sandy wasn't too bothered, and although called upon to work very hard, he revelled in every moment, even when asked to go aloft. He was learning all the time.

Repairs to the ship held good, though when there were high winds, and Sandy was swinging on his hammock, he couldn't help wonder at the creak of the repaired mast, and at just how long it would last. Nevertheless they put in without mishap at Plymouth Sound, where as before the captain and first mate went ashore and made the necessary arrangements. Once the ship was berthed, the officers and soldiers disembarked, and the cargo was unloaded (a task Jim and Sandy helped with this time). Thereafter most of the crew were given shore leave. Jim said that he planned to call on relatives, and that Sandy was welcome to come along if he wished. He declined, preferring to do some sightseeing round Plymouth, though he didn't tell Jim his main intention was to visit the naval barracks at Devonport. He had heard from one of the ship's crew, who hailed from Plymouth, that they were recruiting there for young and able-bodied men.

Next morning they went their ways, Jim with his roll of silk tucked away in his kit bag, Sandy with his secret plans. He watched the older man go off in the direction of Stonehouse, while he himself turned and headed for Devonport. At the guardhouse to the barracks he was directed to the recruiting office, where he was made welcome and asked to sit down. He quizzed the officer as to the conditions for joining the Royal Navy. 'You'd be expected,' he was told, 'to carry out normal seaman duties anywhere in the world – in war or peace.' The officer explained that he would start as a B2C rating and would undergo training and service before becoming an ordinary seaman. The main conditions for entry were physical fitness, a reasonable aptitude, and a minimum age of sixteen. He thanked the officer and set off heavy-hearted back towards Plymouth. He was disappointed, of course, at the age requirement, which meant he would have to wait for over six months before he qualified – until April 1893. However, he put it behind him and was determined to enjoy his sightseeing in Plymouth.

From Devonport he walked to Millbay docks, and there watched the fishing boats unload. Then he walked on to the Hoe, to where Francis Drake played bowls before defeating the Armada. From the Hoe he passed the huge stone citadel, and from there carried on to the Barbican. Here he stood and read the inscription on the plaque that commemorated the Pilgrim Fathers.

By now he had had enough of walking, and so made for a nearby alehouse, where he bought himself a meal and a drink. The place was full of seamen whose ships were berthed at the Barbican. He sat in a corner out of sight, listening to the stories being told around him. After a further walk round the Hoe he sat on the grass looking out to the Sound. Later in the evening he returned to the ship, which he found very quiet now that the soldiers had gone and so many of the crew were still away on leave (though some when they did return were the worse for wear from drink). Soon though provisions had been replenished and the ship set sail for Falmouth. With a favourable wind they made good headway along the Cornish coast, entering Falmouth by evening. The ship was anchored and its agent and customs officers rowed out to it, then the latter checked on board for contraband. Later Sandy was called to the captain's cabin, where he was told that the injured seaman he'd replaced had recovered, and was due to return. He added that although Sandy's father had been against him going to sea, he would offer him a job if ever one became available. He was that impressed. Sandy thanked him warmly, saying how grateful he was to have had the opportunity. He paid tribute too to the help he had had from Jim.

Later that evening he said his farewells to Jim and other members of the crew, and returned with the customs officers and ship's agent in their boat to the harbour. There he was met by his brother Joe with the wagon. On the way home Sandy told his brother all about his adventures, not to say the visits to Gibraltar and Plymouth (though he kept quiet about Devonport). Back at the farm he was met with open arms by his mother and Freddie, while his father greeted him only cordially. He said he expected Sandy to knuckle down to the hard work awaiting him, and remarked that in truth he could have done with him back much earlier. For the next two weeks he ground his way through all his outstanding jobs, thoroughly making up for his time away.

Towards the end of his first fortnight back he was told that Tom would be home for the weekend, and that Jim Earle had planned to visit the Richards' farm. Margery had arranged for the four friends to meet up at the old barn on the Saturday afternoon. When that materialised, naturally Sandy had to tell them all about his exciting times abroad, which held them all spellbound. Their own news seemed to pale by comparison. For one brief moment, Sandy was a hero.

Sandy settles back to the farm work and visits Tom's mine and mining school

ALTHOUGH SANDY found it hard after all the excitement of recent times, he soon settled back into his old routine on the farm. For a time he was even content. His mother had looked after the dairy, and Joe had coped with some of his other work while he was away. However, there was plenty still to do. It was only when the workload eased that his thoughts returned to the sea. Then came one weekend in particular that was free of the farm monotony. Tom was home from Redruth and came to see him. He told Sandy he'd arranged for a visit the following Saturday to the mine he was working at, and also a look round the Camborne School of Mines. If he was free, he could come. 'Be glad to,' Sandy said.

The next week was taken up with root-crop deliveries, and on the Saturday he took longer than expected to deliver his milk quota and clean up the dairy afterwards. By the time he got to the Richards' place Jim was already there. Margery was out with the wagon, all set to go, first stop being a visit to her relatives in Redruth, where they had all been invited for a meal. Without further delay they all set off, Margery driving.

When they reached their first appointment they were met at the door by Tom and Margery's uncle and aunt, as well as Tom himself. Uncle George was a tall man with swarthy features, lean-looking, and with brown straight hair that was thinning on top. Aunt Dorothy – or Dolly – was short, tubby, and had slightly bandy legs. Her hair was black and curly, and she was rosy-cheeked as she enjoyed the open air. She was cheerful and had an infectious laugh. The three of them were made to feel welcome.

The four friends sat down to a meal of vegetable soup, Cornish pasties and clotted cream buns. Half an hour or so afterwards, George said it was time for their visit to the mine. Although it wasn't far from the house, they'd use the wagon, as afterwards they'd be going to the school in Camborne. When they got to the mine, George went straight to the captain's office, for permission to take the four visitors round. With that formality over, he led his charges to the main works. In the engine house he explained how the engine operated the stamp-heads and other equipment. They could see the stamp-heads crushing the ore into powder, ready for smelting. The workmen who operated them wore canvas aprons and gloves, and caps to protect their heads. 'They need all that,' said George, 'with so much ore and powder flying about.' Despite that, the workmen's faces were covered in particles of debris.

On actually going down the mine, he showed them the layout of the pump system, designed to bring water up to the surface from the lower levels. Tom showed that he knew about the valves and fittings, because he'd helped to repair them. While they were here, a group of miners appeared, having climbed the ladders from a lower level. They nodded politely. Their clothes were badly worn and covered in dust. Their faces too were covered in dust, and streaked with sweat where they'd wiped them with their hands. They looked very tired. 'No wonder,' said George. 'They'll have been down since early morning.' They were coming up for a break and something to eat and drink.

When George and his visitors had finished their tour they climbed to the surface and returned to the office, where they thanked the captain for allowing them the tour. Tom then drove them to Camborne and the mine school. Here they were greeted by J J Beringer, the principal. Tom introduced those who hadn't met before, then they all set off along a corridor to the first classroom. Here there were rows of bench-like-looking desks, mostly deeply stained with ink, and two of them carved with initials. Tom showed the others where he habitually sat. Sandy looked round, and couldn't help draw attention to the clouds of chalk dust caught in the sunshine streaming in near the blackboard. 'Looks like someone's started to clean up but suddenly disappeared.' Beringer recounted the subjects that were taught.

Next came the library, where there was a strong smell of carbolic. There was an old woman in a corner, with long grey hair, bent double almost, scrubbing the floor. Beringer said hello to her, then showed them a sample of books dealing with scientific subjects. 'We make them available to all the students here,' he said.

Their final look was in the laboratory. Here there were students working at benches, doing their various experiments. Accompanying odours varied from rotten eggs to pear drops to others unspeakably pungent. Beringer, well used to that sort of thing, showed them equipment for analysing tin, copper and other ores. Then he showed them a Brinell testing device for checking the hardness of metals, as well as instruments of chemical experimentation.

With the tour of the school complete, they all thanked Mr Beringer for sparing them the time. George added that Tom was particularly grateful, as a student of the school. Beringer replied that Tom was a good pupil and was destined to do well.

Tom went on ahead of the others and brought the wagon round to the front, and when everyone had climbed on board he drove them back to his aunt and uncle's. There they had an excellent tea. The four friends thanked Dolly and George for their hospitality. Tom, who was not returning with them, walked the three to the wagon, where they said their farewells. Margery took up the reins, and soon they were on their way.

When Sandy got home, the family were in the parlour, having had their evening meal. His parents were pleased he'd enjoyed his day out. What they secretly hoped was excursions like this would help him settle back into the life of the farm, though by now the desire in his breast for the all-alluring sea was unquenchable.

Sandy is ill but recovers to enjoy some time with his friends

AFTER HELPING to build the last of the corn-ricks there was a lull in Sandy's work. For a while he was able to relax a bit and read his books in the evenings, and with more time on his hands dream of the sea and reflect on those exciting times with Jim and the rest of the crew. The lull didn't last long however, as in

October the root crops had to be lifted and taken into storage, and because his father worked him hard and for long hours each day he was less inclined to daydream.

Towards the end of harvesting the weather changed from dry to days of heavy rainfall. Sandy, Joe, their father and some of the farm labourers were now working in mud that stuck to their boots. Sandy was given the most difficult field, the one with the steep slope at the brow of the hill. In the rain and damp, Sandy inevitably caught a cold, and with it a persistent cough and sore throat. He had gathered the crop from the last of the rows, and was trudging uphill through the runnels of mud, his legs shaky and leaden. A last shower of rain had finally soaked him to the skin, with his clothes utterly sodden. By late evening nevertheless he had finished lifting the last of the crop and loading the wagon. He was driven on by sheer determination, a sense that no matter what he would show his father he couldn't be beaten.

He was completely exhausted and ready to drop, but drove the wagon to the storage area near the farmhouse, where some of the hands unloaded it. He went in and told his mother, then working in the kitchen, how drained he felt. 'You look terrible,' she said. 'I'll prepare you a bath while you get out of those things.'

When he'd had his bath he found that his mother had put a warming pan in his bed and a hot drink on his bedside table. His aches were partly eased, but his night was a restless one, disrupted by coughing fits and the soreness of his throat. Next day his mother nursed him with linctus and hot drinks, and it was only after another day of such care that he was able to go down to the kitchen and eat a meal. He didn't get back to work until the following week, and even then he still felt the effects of his illness. Fortunately, by now there was only light work to do and the dairy each day.

At the end of the month he was invited to the Richards'

Halloween party, which he attended but left early, still not feeling fit. By Guy Fawkes' night he felt much better, and as usual he went with Margery and Jim to the Bonallack display. As in previous years there was a good crowd gathered round the bonfire, in the fire's orange light in which Sandy had every opportunity to study the new laced-up boots and cut-away coat that Margery was wearing. He wondered why she had dressed up simply for a firework display, but found out later, when she sought out George Minhinick in the crowd and gave him a wave. He came over. 'You know,' he said, 'I'm all alone. For some reason my friends haven't turned up.'

'Stick with us then,' Margery said.

After the display, more spectacular and colourful than ever before, George invited the three friends back to his house for a mug of soup. They sat about in his warm kitchen, with Sandy at George's prompting talking with great relish all about his Gibraltar experience. 'All thanks to your father,' he said, 'who got me the berth.' George then asked Jim how he liked his job in his father's boatyard. 'It's the best thing in the world,' said Jim, 'especially the training.' George then finally cut to the chase, going on to talk to Margery first about the firework display, then about some of the finer points of animal husbandry, a subject he said he had studied for some years. Jim allowed this to go on for some time, but eventually interrupted, saying he had promised Mrs Richards that Margery would arrive home at a reasonable hour. Rather coyly, Margery accepted it was time to go. The three friends stepped out together to the stable yard, while George stood in the kitchen doorway saying goodnight. His was a special wave for Margery as they drove away.

On their way back to the Richards' farm Sandy kept his counsel, but could see that Margery's thoughts were all with George now, and wondered if this was what had made Jim cross.

Visit of Sandy's uncle and cousin from Gunnislake

IN THE weeks leading to Christmas Sandy was busy both with the dairy and trips to Falmouth, where he took the wagon-loads of vegetables to sell at market. He enjoyed these trips as they gave him the opportunity to visit the harbour. There he would walk along the wall, to see if he could recognise any of the ships berthed. On one such occasion he met Jim Webber, who told him about his latest voyage to Italy and the wonderful architecture he had seen there.

If the weather had been calm and mild in the early part of December, a week before Christmas southern Cornwall was hit by high winds. At night, lying in bed, Sandy could hear the slates rattling on the roof, the drainpipes creaking, or the clatter of loose debris as falling branches took bits of masonry with them. With the wind whistling in the trees, he was reminded of the storm on the crossing to Gibraltar, when there were moments he thought it certain he would lose his life.

On the morning after the worst night, Sandy's father examined the house and the barns for damage. The house was intact, but the roof to one of the barns had suffered slightly. Joe and Sandy were tasked to repair it, after they had done their usual jobs. When he'd finished in the dairy, Sandy collected tools and met his brother at the barn. Joe positioned a long ladder and they both climbed to the roof to survey the damage. Sandy measured the broken timbers and climbed back down to fetch planks. While he was cutting them, Joe removed the broken timber. Between them they soon had the new timber and felt in place, fitted and nailed. Their father examined the repair and pronounced it good and watertight.

Although they had worked together, Sandy and Joe never spoke, other than asking for tools to be passed. So far as Sandy could tell, it was reluctance on Joe's part to make any kind of conversation. He sensed that his brother still bore him a grudge for having to make up for his being away at sea, and so the mood persisted, even into Christmas Day, where as in previous years their mother provided an excellent family feast. There was something hollow about it all however – the ritual, the enforced *bonhomie*, the exchange of presents in the parlour. Sandy received clothes mainly, and as far as giving was concerned had wrapped up many a curio from his trip to the shops in Gibraltar. Joe and his father took these offerings with formality and simple thanks, while Sandy's mother and his youngest brother Freddie were overjoyed.

In the new year there was a letter from Elizabeth's brother Peter in Gunnislake. He had some business in Falmouth and wanted to know if he and his son George could stay at the farm for a couple of days. John wrote back, saying they'd be welcome, and that everyone looked forward to seeing them. For Sandy this was welcome news, as he had thoroughly enjoyed his stay at Gunnislake. They arrived by train at Falmouth, where John and Elizabeth came to collect them. As Elizabeth hadn't seen her brother or nephew for over a year it was quite an emotional reunion.

Back at the farm, uncle and cousin were welcomed rapturously by Joe, Sandy and Freddie. 'My,' said Peter, 'how you've all grown – and Joe here's a dashing young man!'

Sandy said to George he hoped they would spend time together, though for now he was tired after his work and went upstairs with Joe where they washed and changed. When they reappeared they all sat down to a sumptuous meal, after which they retired to the parlour. John said to his brother-in-law: 'I've business myself in Falmouth tomorrow. We could meet up, when you've done yours.'

'Excellent idea.'

'There's a nice hotel where we can have lunch.'

'That sounds very acceptable.' Peter's business was at a solicitor's office.

'Why yes,' said Elizabeth. 'While you're away, Sandy I'm sure you would love to show George round the farm.'

'And I could take him to Falmouth the day after that.'

'That's settled then.'

George shared Sandy's room while his father was in the spare. When they had gone off to bed, the two boys chatted about the good times they'd had together in Gunnislake, until it was George who fell asleep. Sandy couldn't get off himself so quickly, but lay awake thinking and planning. His cousin's visit offered him relief from the coming prospect of all those long winter nights and short dark days – but next April, he thought, he would be sixteen and eligible for the Royal Navy. It seemed a lifetime away.

The next day Sandy showed his cousin George around the farm, then took him up the hill to meet the Richards family. While they were in the kitchen having drinks, Mr Richards asked the new visitor all about Gunnislake, and what job he was doing. George said he was an apprentice joiner who enjoyed his work. His father had advised him not to go into the local mines as many were closing down due to the falling price of tin. 'Interesting,' Richards said.

When they returned home, George and Sandy found that their fathers were back from Falmouth, and judging by their joviality had had a successful day. After their evening meal, the parents retired to the parlour and Sandy and George entertained Freddie. Joe went to his room to read.

The following day, after his early morning milk deliveries, Sandy got Blackie from the stable and hitched him to the wagon, and when George was ready they set off together for Falmouth. There Sandy showed him round the moor, where fairs were held, and last year even a circus. Next they strolled to Trevethen school, where Sandy pointed out the classroom in which he'd done his lessons many years before, and from there they went on to Killigrew Street, where he showed him the house where he was born. After that they drove to the harbour. 'That's Pendennis Castle,' said Sandy on the way.

Along the harbour wall Sandy pointed out the many different types of fishing boat berthed there, as well as naming some of the larger ships. He said, without thinking much about the consequences, that he hoped sooner or later to be back at sea, enjoying the long voyages and visiting so many foreign ports. By now they were hungry, and so tucked into the picnic they had brought, consisting of cooked chicken, bread and fruit, and a nice cold drink. After that they returned to the farm. There George found his father in the parlour reading letters he had picked up from the solicitor. 'You had a good day?' he asked his son. George mentioned the moor, the castle and the harbour, and innocently related Sandy's expectations of going to sea. Later Peter casually mentioned this to his brother-in-law, who contained his shock and betrayed no feelings on the matter at all. In reality, he was furious.

The next day the three brothers said their farewells, as their mother and father took their guests from Gunnislake back to the station, where it was all hugs, handshakes and promises to keep in touch.

Sandy runs away from home and joins the Royal Navy

WITH THE train was out of sight, John and his wife left the station and returned to the horse and carriage. Before driving off he told her of Sandy's intentions. She could see that he was angry, but pleaded with him not to lose his temper when they got back home, but to try to reason with their son. Despite that, she still foresaw the outcome.

John drove very fast, and on getting to the farm asked his wife to tell Joe to stable, feed and water the horse. He himself set off for the dairy, where Sandy was at work. Sandy could see he was livid. So, now came the spectacle of John Toye accusing his son of underhand behaviour, with his secret plans for a life at sea. Sandy tried to explain that he had done his best to make a go of the farm work, but was unhappy. John simply wouldn't listen, and accused him of being underhand and ungrateful to his parents. The argument got quite heated, and came close to blows. Luckily Sandy's mother appeared and stood between them. She was in tears and told them to stop. John turned on his heels, went off in a huff and slammed the door behind him. Elizabeth meanwhile tried to pacify her son, but he was too upset to listen and locked himself in his room. For several days he avoided his father, seeing him only at meal times. His mother tried to reconcile the two, but that was only futile. After some days of this, and after careful deliberation, Sandy decided he would run away from home the next time his father stayed overnight at Truro.

With that as his plan, Sandy arranged for an urgent meeting the following weekend with his three friends at the barn. Margery got it organised, and the meeting took place on the following Saturday afternoon. Prior to that, Sandy discovered that his father would be visiting Truro on the morning of the 27th of January. He talked the whole thing over with his friends, and gave Margery a farewell letter to pass on to his mother – though not until several days after he had gone.

'What do you think you'll do?' Margery asked.

'I'll lie about my age, and might get accepted into the Royal Navy.' If he failed at that he would try for a berth as seaman on one of the ships calling in at Plymouth. They all looked so sad at this, and said how sorry they were he was going. But it was worse than that. Because of the rift between him and his father he would never be allowed back home after he'd run away. 'I want to make a pact,' he said. 'I want us to meet up here in the barn ten years from now.' They all agreed to that. Sandy added that he would write to Margery from time to time, and to his mother, once it was not possible for him to be brought back. It was a sad parting.

On the evening his father left for Truro Sandy secretly packed his bag and pocketed some money he had saved. Early the next morning he dressed quickly and quietly crept downstairs. As he left the farmhouse he looked back and thought about some of the happy times he had had in previous years. He would miss his mother and young Freddie desperately, but he felt he had to go away if ever he was to be master of his own destiny. He got off quickly, lest his mother heard him moving around, and struck out along the road to Falmouth, thrilled at the sense of freedom and the crisp early morning, with its clear winter sky. At the station he bought a single ticket for Plymouth, and before long there was a train from Penzance. When he climbed in, there were still only a few other passengers. That meant there was less of a chance that Sandy would be recognised.

On disembarking at North Road station he went immediately to a baker's shop and bought himself something to eat. He then walked to Devonport, where he booked into a lodging house (just in case he was rejected by the recruitment officer). After settling in he went to the naval barracks, but on making enquiries at the guardhouse was told that the recruiting officer was away that day, and would be back tomorrow. At that he was disappointed.

He found a pub and bought a drink and hot pies. No one questioned his age. After that he went to Millbay Docks and checked what fishing boats and ships were in, fully intending to find a berth (in the event that his application for the navy didn't succeed). Then he walked around the Hoe before returning to his lodging house, where he went to bed early. Next morning he made his way to the barracks. At the main gate he saw the duty Petty Officer, who directed him to the recruiting office.

There the officer recognised him from his previous visit and sat him down near his desk. He asked him his date of birth. Sandy kept a straight face as he said the 10th of December 1876 – four months before his actual date of birth – which the officer accepted. He then had to give details of his schooling and undergo a medical, which he passed. After that he was told he had satisfied the statutory conditions for entry, and was asked to fill in a form. That done, the officer shook his hand. 'Tomorrow morning,' he said, 'you must go along to the seamen's quarters and report to Chief Petty Officer Driscoll.'

Next morning Sandy settled his bill at the lodging house and made his way to the barracks. At the main gate, having produced a copy of his signing-on form, he was directed to the seamen's quarters. Here he found Chief Petty Officer Driscoll, who took his form and led him to the store, where he was measured and given his uniform. After a brief settling-in period he was taken to HMS *Ganges*, the training ship, and thus his career in the Royal Navy began.

Some weeks later he wrote to Margery, and received a very prompt reply. She said that his mother and brother Freddie had been very upset, and that his father had made numerous enquiries at the harbour in Falmouth, all to no avail, and so had given up trying to find out what had happened to him. He waited until after his sixteenth birthday, then wrote several times to his mother. He received only one letter back, in which she said she'd been very upset at what he'd done. She did however wish him every success in the Royal Navy. She couldn't write again, she said, as it caused so much friction with his father.

Sandy corresponded with Margery for about a year after that, but lost touch with her when he went into service on HMS *Aurora*, which left Plymouth for duties overseas.

The passage of time and ten years later

DURING THE next ten years Sandy enjoyed a contented but disciplined life in the Royal Navy. It was a complete change in his fortunes, transforming the drudgery of farm routine – with its scant financial reward – to adventures overseas, visiting ports in many foreign climes. After training on HMS *Ganges* he served on several warships – such as *Impregnable*, *Aurora*, *Dreadnought*, *Vivid* and *Cambridge* – to name just some. He visited the ports of Naples and Genoa. On one of his tours a ship he served on called in at Simonstown, so that Sandy was able to visit Cape Town and see the flat-top, steep-sided Table Mountain.

What thrilled him most as a young sailor were the visits to Hong Kong and Shanghai, whose culture was so different from that of Britain. He was enchanted with all the unusual things he saw: the pagodas with upturned roofs, the exotic use of colour in the clothes people wore and the buildings they inhabited. Sometimes he just couldn't believe that an ordinary farm boy could even begin to experience the sheer opulence of the Orient. Also it filled him with delight to stand on the deck of a huge warship, bristling with guns, and cutting through the water at high speed, when to him the clank of the steam engines and the swish of the waves as they passed underneath were music to the ears.

With hard work and a willingness to shoulder responsibility Sandy gradually received promotion, until in his tenth year he was made a Petty Officer. This gave him status and security financially. Throughout that time, with no further letters from his mother, he slowly accepted his family as just a distant memory. However, towards the end of 1902, while serving on HMS *Medea*, Sandy's thoughts began to turn to his pact with his childhood friends, and with that in mind he organised some shore leave. He wrote to Margery and asked her if she could arrange for Jim Earle and her brother Tom and herself to meet him. She wrote back promptly, saying she would do her best, though if the others couldn't make it, she certainly would. Several days prior to the reunion, Sandy caught a train from Plymouth to Falmouth and booked in to a hotel near the station.

At the hotel the manager recognised him, as he had been in the same class at grammar school. After they had reminisced, Sandy explained the reason for his visit, and why he had run away from home and joined the Royal Navy. His old classmate was so taken that Sandy had returned to honour the pact that he offered him the use of his pony and trap, for his visit to the Richards' farm. On the day of the visit itself he went for a walk round the harbour first, where the fishing boats and ships tied up at anchor brought back many a happy memory. When, slightly nervously, he eventually set off for the farm, he made sure he drove there slowly, not wishing to arrive earlier than agreed. He stopped at the bottom of the hill below the Richards' farm, and there tethered the horse to a tree. Before going up the hill he took a long lingering look at what used to be his home. He shrugged and sighed and continued on his way.

He approached the old barn, the same Sandy of old but now in his Petty Officer's uniform, his boots polished and his buttons bright. Suddenly his three friends came out from inside and ran towards him, and embraced him one by one. Then they all went and sat down inside. Margery was a fine-looking woman, if a little overweight. Tom and Jim were mature and fit, but were lined and furrowed with life's responsibilities. 'So, what have you all been doing with yourselves?' Sandy said.

Margery, who in her letters had not told him much about herself, was now Mrs Minhinick, having got married to George. Their son William was three years old. George's father had gifted them a farm after their wedding, and after many years of cattle breeding they had one of the best herds in Cornwall. Tom was now deputy to the captain of the mine, where he had worked for nearly twelve years, having passed his exams and got his engineering certificates. Jim was now in charge of his father's boat-building yard in Falmouth, and as well as building fishing boats he designed yachts for very wealthy businessmen.

The three friends now turned to Sandy and asked him to tell them about *his* life. He mentioned the warships he had served on, and all the foreign ports he had visited. He dwelt on his visits to Hong Kong and Shanghai, these being to him the most fascinating ports he had ever seen. In the last three years he had become expert in all aspects of gunnery in warships. Lastly he told them that he'd written to his mother saying when he would be in Falmouth and at what hotel, but she hadn't replied. There was nothing they could say. Before leaving them he embraced them all again, and as he walked down the hill he shouted back: 'See you again in *another* ten years – when, that is, I'll be a captain.'

He collected the horse and trap at the bottom of the hill and drove back to the hotel. Sitting in the lounge after his evening meal he felt it had been a privilege to see his friends after so long a time. He was grateful to Margery who had done so much to bring the four of them together. Next morning after breakfast he went for a walk round Falmouth, revisiting the places he'd known as a child. It would be his last full day, as the following morning he was to catch the train to Plymouth and rejoin his ship. After lunch he sat down in the lounge for a quiet read of the paper. So absorbed, he heard a knock at the door, and thought it must be the manager. However, walking slowly towards him across the room was his mother, the tears streaming down her cheeks, and her arms outstretched. He embraced her, speechless, but bursting with joy that his mother had come to see him at last. In the doorway were Margery and his youngest brother Freddie, now a tall young man of almost twenty, beaming irrepressibly.

Years later

SANDY RETIRED from the Royal Navy in 1919, having risen to the rank of Chief Petty Officer. After managing several businesses he purchased the Park Inn Hotel in Penzance in the 1920s, and settled there with his family for many years.